"This book is some of the fruit of God's Spirit in a woman who loves him and His people deeply. Nada has been able to capture the depth and riches of the Scriptures yet helps us reflect on them in a way that enriches our walk with the Lord wherever we are at. It integrates head and heart. It encourages us to be real with God as we interact with His Word and seek to apply it to our lives. I pray that this resource will be a great encouragement to many as we live in an ever changing world but need our roots to grow deeply into God's love. I'm excited to see how Nada is using her gifts and learning and love to build up God's people."

Rev Jackie Stoneman
(former principal Mary Andrews College)

Forty years of
Thankfulness

Cultivating *thankfulness* in times of suffering

NADA APPLEBY

Ark House Press
arkhousepress.com

Cataloguing in Publication Data:
Title: Forty Years of Thankfulness
ISBN: 978-0-6489380-6-4 (pbk.)
Subjects: Biography; Devotional;
Other Authors/Contributors: Appleby, Nada

Design and layout by initiateagency.com

Foreword

I began writing *Forty Years of Thankfulness* the year I turned forty. It was a hard year of painful lessons; at the time I found myself diving into the Bible to find some solace, perhaps some wisdom in how to move forward; I felt stuck. I sat alongside the Psalms each day and traced the history of the promised Messiah throughout the Scriptures. During that year I wept, laughed and wrote music to the Lord Jesus expressing his goodness to me. He brought me through a truly difficult time and gave me joy instead of bitterness.

We all experience trials and difficult seasons but I have reached the conclusion from the Scriptures that God intends to use them for his glory and our ultimate good. It's not sinful to cry out and feel the painful emotions that come with suffering; it's what makes us human. But perhaps what distinguishes a Christian from a non-Christian is *who* they cry out to. The Psalmists shared their own suffering; they expressed the deep anguish and bitterness of living in a broken world; yet they held onto their wonderful God, their Creator, Redeemer and Deliverer. They cried out to Him and he heard them.

When God rescued his people from terrible suffering in Egypt, they held onto their fears and continued to complain and express their bitterness. They continued to dwell on the past. They blamed God instead of seeing him as their Saviour, and ultimately, they missed out on a wonderful future with him. That year, God moved me to spend more time in the Word; I journaled, I prayed, I wrote music and I gathered with Christian friends and shared my difficult thoughts and feelings. In time God used all of this to cultivate a love for the Lord Jesus like I had in the beginning, love for his people grew and I experienced a wonderful peace that God was with me and for me.

Instead of grumbling like the Israelites did in the wilderness for forty years, I found myself giving thanks to God for sending Jesus to die for me. When Jesus said "I have come that they may have life and have it to the full" (John 10:10), he was speaking about the life that endures for all of eternity. It is a wonderful, gracious act of God that he chooses us to be included in his family history and my hope is that you might find your place amongst Christian friends and travel together with them on the journey towards our heavenly home, acknowledging all that God has done through our trials, yet pressing on to take hold of Christ (Phil. 3:13).

There are many Christian devotionals that can help us to engage with the Scriptures. This Bible reading guide helps readers follow the overarching story of the Bible so as to begin to understand the breadth and depth of the gospel, the good news of Jesus Christ. Some of the readings are longer than others. This is purposeful. Please don't skip them, instead take longer in these readings. This is not a 40-day devotional, it could be stretched over 40 weeks or 40 years! This could be a great study for a small group to use and explore or for one-to-one discipleship.

It is my desire and prayer that you might be encouraged and strengthened in your Christian faith and that you are spurred on to share the wonderful news of Jesus with others. Please pray before you begin, as you read and afterwards. I have included mine as a guide, you might resonate with them or you can pray your own prayers that are relevant for your own life. The Bible contains the knowledge of the greatest treasure you could ever imagine so please don't rush. Spend some time getting to know the One who knows everything there is to know about you.

It is my prayer for you just like the Apostle Paul that:

"Out of his glorious riches he may strengthen you with power through his Spirit in your inner being, so that Christ may dwell in your hearts through faith. And I pray that you, being rooted and established in love, may have power, together with all the Lord's holy people, to grasp how wide and long and high and deep is the love of Christ, and to know this love that surpasses knowledge - that you may be filled to the measure of all the fullness of God."

(Eph. 3:16-19)

Grace and peace in Jesus's name

Nada

Acknowledgements

Forty Years of Thankfulness was a labour of love that I could not have begun or completed without the help of my loving God. I am thankful to him for opening the eyes of my heart to see the wonderful truth of the gospel and for the many women that he has placed in my life that have spurred me on in my Christian faith. Thank you to Jackie and Kerrie for encouraging me in my studies at Mary Andrews College and sparking a love for learning to love others through listening. For the faithful saints at Port Kembla and Warrawong Anglican Church who taught me humility. For Maureen, who undertook the task of editing and turning my feeble words into something print-worthy. For Ness and Alison for ensuring I remained faithful to the Bible. For Margaret, who taught me the value of memorising God's word. For dear Shirley who imparted her love of God's word into my life over the fence. For Heidi who encouraged me with her zeal for the Lord! And for my mum Leony, who continues to teach me the value of grace and truth.

Contents

Contents

To my sons: may you resolve to trust and follow Jesus and love him with all of your heart, mind, soul and strength.
Love Mummy

1

Beginning

Readings: Genesis 1-2, Psalm 139, John 1:1-18

FROM THE VERY BEGINNING, LIFE was dependent on God. No life appeared on the earth until God sent the rain, the whole surface of the earth was flowing with streams of life and then God made man, from the dust of the earth, he breathed into man's nostrils the breath of life and he became a living being. God created mankind in his own image and he blessed them, commanding them to "Be fruitful and increase in number" (Gen. 1:28). God provided for them; giving them every seed-bearing plant and every tree that had fruit with seed in it (Gen. 1:29). God gave them abundance and the responsibility to 'rule' over the fish in the sea, the birds in the sky and over *every* living creature that moves on the ground (Gen. 1:28-29).

God planted his people in a garden full of life and it was good. In the middle of the garden amongst an abundance of trees there were two trees: there was the tree of life and the tree of the knowledge of good and evil (Gen. 2:9); watered by a river which flowed across the ancient plains from Eden (Gen. 2:10). God had one rule for the man "You are free to eat from any tree in the garden; but you must not eat from the tree of the knowledge of good and evil, for when you eat from it you will certainly die" (Gen. 2:16-17). Of course, for the man at this point, death and its consequences were a great mystery, but to the author of Genesis, death was all pervading. One might imagine the anticipation of a grief about to unravel in the garden. Yet life in all its array surrounded man and he was given, on top of all this goodness, a helper, a wife, and they became one (Gen. 2:24).

David's prayer to God, written down in Psalm 139, reflects the wondrous event of life that begins in a mother's womb. He said "I praise you because I am fearfully and wonderfully made; your works are wonderful, I know that full well" (Ps. 139:14). God longs to give life, he is indeed a wonderful Creator who loves us dearly and watches over us even in our mother's womb. Indeed, this is exactly why Jesus was sent; God longed for our lives to be watered by his streams of living water. Jesus said "Let anyone who is thirsty come to me and drink. Whoever believes in me, as the Scripture has said, rivers of living water will flow from within them" (Jn. 7:37-38). Reminiscent of Eden, Jesus is the new river that waters the garden, He is the true source of everlasting life.

Prayer: *Heavenly Father, it is difficult to imagine the perfect place that you created for your people in the beginning. When I gaze upon a beautiful sunset or stand up on a mountain, it is just a hint of your glory. You gave your people in the beginning everything they needed to live a purposeful, everlasting life, with you. Please search me God and know my heart, please see if there is any offensive way in me and lead me in the way everlasting. Amen.*

My thoughts, feelings and questions from the readings...

_____

_____

_____

_____

_____

_____

_____

_____

_____

_____

_____

_____

_____

2

Trust

Readings: Genesis 3, Psalm 51, Colossians 1-2

For a time, nakedness in the garden was normal, there was no shame (Gen. 2:25). God's people had been given a vast array of food to eat but the wild animals were limited to the 'green plants' (Gen. 1:30). One fateful day, one of these wild animals, the Snake, spoke to Eve encouraging her to question God's goodness; "You will not certainly die…For God knows that when you eat from it your eyes will be opened, and you will be like God, knowing good and evil" (Gen. 3:4-5). The seed of doubt was sown and Eve, seeing that the fruit could not only give her sustenance but also wisdom, made the decision to take and eat (Gen. 3:6). And without hesitation she shared the fruit with her husband (Gen. 3:6).

Adam and Eve's perfect trust in God for provision, protection and wisdom was broken. Now, with eyes wide open, feelings of shame entered their life and they hid in fear (Gen. 3:7-8). The Snake's strategy had seemingly worked quite easily. He had successfully cast doubt and twisted God's Word just enough so, that the decision Eve made seemed reasonable enough. The wisdom of the snake appeared trustworthy and yet it led to disastrous consequences still felt today. God's people could no longer walk in the garden with God himself (Gen. 3:8) or taste the abundant provision. Freedom to access the tree of life was now blocked. They would now need to till the ground and work in order to provide for themselves (Gen. 3:18-19). They would wrestle with sin until the day they would die (Gen. 3:15). God's protection was lost, the Snake that they were commanded to rule over (Gen. 1:28), now had rule over them. Of course, the Snake's strategies have not changed, he does not have the creativity that God has. He still tries to flaunt his wisdom causing doubt amongst God's people.

The apostle Paul knew his strategies all too well. In fact, when he prayed for the Christians at Colossae, he prayed that they might be continually filled with the "knowledge of his will through all wisdom and understanding that the Spirit gives" (Col. 1:9). The spirit of the Snake had infiltrated 'the church' in order to cast doubt again over God's word. Paul warned them "see to it that no one takes you captive through hollow and deceptive philosophy, which depends on human tradition and the elemental spiritual forces of this world rather than on Christ" (Col. 2:8). They were at risk of losing the abundant provision made through Christ by listening to false wisdom. Paul encourages the Christians at Colossae and Laodicea to remain in Christ, to continue to set their hearts and minds on things above and, continue to give thanks for Jesus for rescuing them from darkness and bringing them into the light. They were to cling to the gospel message until Jesus returned.

Prayer: *Heavenly Father, thank you that you love me, that you were not content to let me die. In your great mercy you sent your son Jesus so that I might not take the punishment for my disobedience. Father though there are natural consequences when I sin, please help me to trust that I am forgiven and set free from the eternal consequences of sin. Please help me to trust in your wisdom and understanding. Please help me to obey your word and live a life that is pleasing to you, one that bears everlasting fruit. Amen.*

My thoughts, feelings and questions from the readings...

_____

_____

_____

_____

_____

_____

_____

_____

_____

_____

_____

_____

_____

_____

3

Taken

Readings: Genesis 6-9, Isaiah 54, Matthew 24

WHEN GOD SAW HOW GREAT the sin of the human race had become his heart became deeply troubled and he regretted that he had made human beings (Gen. 6:5-6). The Creation that he had breathed life into in the beginning was now about to be taken away. God saw the unfaithfulness of the people of Noah's time and decided to put an end 'to all people' (Gen. 6:13). He is a God of action and will not allow sin to go unpunished. This theme will continue to surface throughout the Old Testament as the sin of mankind continues to fester. And yet God chose by grace to preserve a family and a remnant of every kind of creature and Noah does everything just as God commanded him (Gen. 6:22).

The story of Noah reminds me of the words Jesus spoke whilst sitting on the Mount of Olives; He talked to his disciples about a time that was coming that resembled the time of Noah, when he would return in full glory in the final judgement. Jesus said to them to be ready because long ago, "in the days before the flood, people were eating and drinking, marrying and giving in marriage...and they knew nothing about what would happen until the flood came and took them all away" (Matt. 24:37-39). People were just going on with the business they called life but they were unaware that their life was ebbing away.

When we gaze at the sight of a beautiful rainbow after a deluge of rain, creation points to the covenant God made with Noah and his family and every living creature at that time, promising to never send a great flood again to wipe out the living (Gen. 9:10-11). Whilst God judges the sins of mankind, redemption is available to those who he declares righteous. When Jesus sat with his disciples, he was pointing to a time, just as God spoke through the prophet Isaiah, to a day when Jesus would return in full glory to judge and to redeem. Let us be a people who are ready for that day just as Noah was. Let us not delay in coming to Christ the redeemer for forgiveness, that he might extend his mercy and peace and preserve our life for all of eternity.

Prayer: *Heavenly Father, thank you that your judgements are just and that you are a God who acts and deals with sin. Please forgive me for the stubbornness in my own heart. Please help me to hear your voice and obey your commands just like Noah. Please help me to trust in Jesus, the one who was perfectly obedient to your commands and through him gave life to all who place their trust in him. Amen.*

My thoughts, feelings and questions from the readings…

_____

_____

_____

_____

_____

_____

_____

_____

_____

_____

_____

_____

_____

_____

_____

_____

4

Blessed

Readings: Genesis 12-15, Psalm 105, Hebrews 11

J UST AS GOD BLESSED NOAH and his sons and commanded them to "Be fruitful and increase in number and fill the earth" (Gen. 9:1). Now he had chosen Abram, the beginning of God's family, to bless, but instead of commanding Abram to 'increase in number', this time it would be God who does the work. He would make Abram's family into a great nation (Gen. 12:2). He would be the one who makes Abram's name great (Gen. 12:2). He would be the one to bless all people through Abram (Gen. 12:3). By faith, Abram listened to God's promises and in obedience, left his country, his people and his home to journey to a land chosen by God (Gen. 12:1), a land promised to his offspring forever (Gen. 12:7, 13:14-15, 15:18-21).

As Abram journeyed closer to the promised land God affirmed his steps through not only the blessing of Melchizedek, King of Salem (Gen. 14:19), but also his very own presence (Gen. 15:1). Though Abram's life was blessed, the future of his family in the distant future would be plagued with darkness (Gen. 15:13). Even though a time of suffering would come for God's chosen family, God assured Abram that he would deliver judgement on the nation that they would serve for four hundred years and he would bring them out (Gen. 15:13-14). Abraham waited another twenty-five years before his son Isaac was born; the promised son.

During that time of patient endurance, God strengthened and sanctified Abram for the task ahead. He gave him a new name: 'Abraham'. This was the beginning of a royal family (Gen. 17:6). Abraham's patient endurance is an encouragement to me because I don't like waiting. I am often tempted to question God and his timing and wonder why he is not acting quicker in a particular circumstance. Abraham is commended for his faith, because he waited patiently for a promise he would not see perfectly fulfilled in his lifetime. His confidence was based on the unseen and the evidence of his faith was seen through his obedience.

Prayer: *Heavenly Father, thank you that you fulfilled your promises to Abraham through Jesus. Father thank you that the promises have extended to me and my family. Father, I confess that sometimes I find it very difficult to wait. Please forgive me and assure me in those times that the gift of your Word and your Spirit are enough, that you are trustworthy and always working for my good. Amen.*

My thoughts, feelings and questions from the readings...

_____

_____

_____

_____

_____

_____

_____

_____

_____

_____

_____

_____

_____

5

Provision

Readings: Genesis 22-28, Isaiah 53, 1 Peter 1

I SAAC'S BIRTH WAS THE BEGINNING of the fulfilment of God's promises to Abraham and we learn that trial and testing mark Isaac's life so that God's faithfulness could be revealed. We learn of the time his father took him up a mountain and laid him on an altar (Gen. 22:9) preparing to slay him at God's command. It is unfathomable that a parent would willingly offer up their only child to God in obedience. And yet perhaps it provides a glimpse of what God would one day demand from the Son of Man to make atonement for sins.

Though Abraham and Isaac were considered faithful, God knew that the generations to follow would be unfaithful. God would ultimately be the one that who would sacrifice his only Son whom He loved, for the sake of the whole world. In this moment, God's perfect provision was evident in the appearance of a ram to be slain instead and Isaac was saved (Gen. 22:13). Amidst the suffering of Isaac losing his mother Sarah, God provided again for his family through a wife for him: Rebekah, whom he loved (Gen. 24:67). Faith and patience are again apparent in God's chosen family as they wait for children of their own.

Twenty years pass before his sons, Esau and Jacob (Gen. 25:25-26) are born and so the promised family of Abraham continued to grow and they indeed became as numerous as the stars in the sky. Esau though, was a source of grief for Isaac and Rebekah (Gen. 26:35) and though he was deservedly entitled to the blessing of the firstborn, in God's Sovereignty, it was Jacob, the second born, who received the blessing (Gen. 28:1) and the blessing was affirmed by God in the renewal of the promises first given to Abraham (Gen. 28:13-15).

God confirmed his complete commitment to his word and assured Jacob of his continual presence (Gen. 28:15). The faith of the patriarchs: Abraham, Isaac and Jacob, were proved genuine. God continued to bring his promises to bear through their lives. Though Peter's first letter was written after the coming of the Messiah, his letter was written during a time of testing for the early Christians. He teaches them to not be surprised, the testing is necessary so that the Spirit at work in their life through faith can be proved genuine. Genuine faith in Jesus Christ results in 'inexpressible and glorious joy' in the midst of trials because it is a sign that they are saved (1 Pet. 1:8-9). It is God's power and faithfulness that is at work in Christians who are able to endure suffering and still give praise to God.

Prayer: *Heavenly Father, thank you that in love you have provided all that is necessary to live a godly life. Father thank you for your unwavering commitment to your word given to Abraham, Isaac and Jacob. Thank you that even though we are undeserving of your love, the vows you made to your people were trustworthy and fulfilled through the sacrifice of your only Son Jesus. Thank you for your active presence in the lives of those who trust in your Son and that even in suffering, you can cause a Christian's heart to overflow with thankfulness. Amen.*

My thoughts, feelings and questions from the readings...

_____

_____

_____

_____

_____

_____

_____

_____

_____

_____

_____

_____

_____

_____

FORTY YEARS OF THANKFULNESS

6

Family

Readings: Genesis 29-35, Psalm 33, 1 Peter 2

J ACOB CONTINUED ON HIS JOURNEY east and stopped at a well no-
ticing three flocks of sheep being watered by it (Gen. 29:2). While
speaking with the shepherds, Rachel came with the fourth flock
and he realised that she was part of his family. She was beautiful
and Jacob wept with joy with the knowledge that she was his own flesh
and blood. He fell in love and was willing to serve her father seven years
and then another, in return for Rachel (Gen. 29:18). But God had chosen
her sister Leah for Jacob, to be the mother of Reuben, Simeon, Levi and
Judah (Gen. 29:31-35).

Jealousy and anger, fuelled by Rachel's impatience, caused her to
shout out to Jacob "give me children, or I'll die!" (Gen. 30:1) and she
took matters into her own hands by offering her servant Bilhah to bear
children for her and, as a result, sons Dan and Naphtali are born to
Bilhah. (Gen. 30:6-8). Now Leah, growing impatient and desiring more
children, offered her servant Zilpah to Jacob, and Gad and Asher were
born - even more sons (Gen. 30:10-13). Leah bore another son Issachar,
then Zebulun. After six sons she finally gave birth to a daughter, Dinah

(Gen. 30:21). In God's time he heard Rachel and enabled her to give birth to a son, Joseph (Gen. 30:22-24).

Not content with just one son, Rachel asked for another, but it was through the birth of Ben-Oni, later named Benjamin by Jacob, that Rachel died (Gen. 35:18). So now, just as the four flocks were watered by one well, through four women, Jacob's family was complete, but it was not without pain, difficulty, grief and anguish with each of their names reflective of the circumstances they were brought into. God worked through the struggles and difficulties of a blended family to bring about the continuing of his promises and thus the beginning of the nation of Israel (Gen. 32:28), a people chosen by grace. God's faithfulness to this family is an encouragement to me when relationships either within my own family or the people of God, are strained. It's a wonderful reminder that our fallen relationships cannot thwart God's plans.

Prayer: *Heavenly Father, thank you that you worked through sinful people to fulfil your promises to Abraham. Thank you for your great mercy and patience shown to me through sending your Son, Jesus. Please help me to wait patiently as I seek your guidance; help me not to rush ahead. Thank you that when I do rush ahead and take matters into my own hands, you continue to bring about your purposes in me. Thank you that your plans never fail. Amen.*

My thoughts, feelings and questions from the readings...

_____

_____

_____

_____

_____

_____

_____

_____

_____

_____

_____

_____

_____

_____

FORTY YEARS OF THANKFULNESS

7

Exalted

Readings: Genesis 37, Psalm 2, Acts 6-7

THE STRUGGLES OF ABRAHAM'S FAMILY continued and the rivalry between the four women extended to the children. Joseph, at seventeen years old, was a shepherd like his mother, and Israel loved him more than his other sons (Gen. 37:3). His brothers knew this and they hated him for it (Gen. 37:4). Their hatred grew for Joseph as he shared his God-given gift; dreams that prophesied to a time when he would 'reign' over them (Gen. 37:8). It seemed that even throughout biblical history the sinful attitude that we see in our children, indeed in ourselves; was at the heart of his brothers' thoughts. Their feelings of hatred and jealousy towards Joseph led to grave sin as they plotted to kill Joseph (Gen. 37:18).

The brothers sold him to a caravan of Ishmaelites from Midian (Gen. 37:28) and Joseph was taken to Egypt as a slave and eventually sold to Potiphar (Gen. 37:36). In the meantime, the brothers lied and told Jacob that some wild animal had killed him. It seems that the time of great suffering had come for Jacob as he mourned the death of his firstborn to Rachel (Gen. 37:35). By all appearances it seemed as though

Joseph was dead, his short life over, and yet God was working through all those struggles not to save just Joseph but to save an entire nation. In the years to follow Joseph would be thrown into prison and then raised to reign over the whole land of Egypt (Gen. 41:41) just as his dreams had prophesied. Joseph suffered the consequences of his brothers' sins and yet God was with him.

Stephen, one of the earliest Christian believers shared this wonderful history of the Israelites with his own Jewish brothers and, just like Joseph, they hated him and plotted in their minds to kill him. Moments before he was stoned to death he recounted, before his enemies, the coming of the Messiah traced throughout the history of God's faithfulness to Abraham, Isaac, Jacob and the twelve patriarchs. Stephen spoke of the famine that forced Jacob's entire family to move to Egypt for food and protection (Acts 7:15).

It was during that time of protection that the Israelites were able to flourish and grow in number (Ex. 1:7). Whilst Egypt signified a place of comfort and protection for the Israelites, after Joseph's generation died, a new king came to power and enslaved God's people. Their lives became bitter and they cried out to God for help (Ex. 2:23). God heard their groans and remembered his promise to Abraham (Ex. 2:24). God had not forgotten his people, he had already sent a saviour to bring them out, a baby marked for death, yet saved by an Egyptian princess (Ex. 2:10). His name was Moses.

Though Stephen was marked for death, his testimony led to the salvation of many and set a time in motion when the gospel could begin its journey out to the nations (Acts 8:4-5), a time of exodus for God's chosen people all over again, but now not just for the Jewish people but the Gentiles as well. As a young Christian Stephen's martyrdom moved me to tears. Stephen was well aware that Jesus had fulfilled the words of Psalm 2, that those who take refuge in him are indeed truly blessed. But from my own human perspective it seemed terribly unfair that he was stoned simply for his belief in Christ as the Messiah. The way he responded in great suffering proved that the gospel had permeated Stephen's entire life and this encourages me to surrender all for the sake of Christ, no matter the cost.

Prayer: *Heavenly Father, it is difficult to be joyful in times of intense suffering. Thank you that even through trials and persecution, this is the way you grow your people. Thank you for Stephen's faith, thank you for his testimony- that he was willing to die for the cause of Christ. Please help me to overcome the struggles life brings with a deep joy and knowledge that all things work together for the good of those who love you. Thank you that our comfort abounds in knowing Christ. Amen.*

My thoughts, feelings and questions from the readings...

_____

_____

_____

_____

_____

_____

_____

_____

_____

_____

_____

_____

_____

_____

_____

8

Messiah

Readings: Exodus 1-4, Psalm 90, 2 Corinthians 1

ONE OF THE GREAT STORIES shared in Sunday school is the story of Moses. As a mother myself, I can only imagine the sheer desperation his mother must have felt as she coated a papyrus basket with tar and pitch, praying that God would somehow save her three-month-old baby. A seemingly impossible situation, yet by faith, she placed him in the reeds of the Nile River and by some miracle he was found by Pharaoh's daughter and later raised by a family that hated his very people (Ex. 2:10).

As Moses grew, the call on his life grew also; and observing the injustice towards his people at age forty; and having an innate desire to rescue them; he sought to bring about justice by killing an Egyptian, and in fear of Pharaoh fled from Egypt into the desert. After another forty years had passed, Moses heard the call of God from the flames of a burning bush, the same place he would later receive the Law and worship God (Ex. 3:12). Moses had been chosen by God to be sent to Egypt to bring God's people out with the promise that God will be with him (Ex.

3:12). It is at this moment that we learn of God's name "I AM WHO I AM", Yahweh (Ex. 3:14), the God of the Abrahamic covenant.

As a young Christian, I mostly remembered Moses as the little baby placed in the reeds or the one who parted the Red Sea or the man coming down from a mountain with the Ten Commandments. I remembered him as a great prophet, a holy man with great power. Yet he was not chosen for his physical strength; after all he was a frail eighty-year old man before God appeared to him. He was not chosen for his power to persuade; even Moses admitted to his shortcomings in this area (Ex. 4:1; and 4:10). He was not chosen for his powerful faith in God because even when God affirmed that he would be the one speaking through Moses, he still pleaded "please send someone else" (Ex. 4:13). Surely it was by sheer grace that Moses was chosen, becoming an earthly vessel for God to accomplish his purposes, pointing forward to a time when Jesus would arrive into the world as a vulnerable baby and grow up with the call of God on his life, as the Messiah, - the one who would redeem his people from slavery and bring them into a glorious relationship with God once again.

Prayer: *Heavenly Father, thank you for remembering your covenant to Abraham. Thank you for hearing the groans of your people and sending a rescuer to deliver them. Thank you for choosing me and sending Jesus to rescue and deliver me to safety. Please help me to hear your call on my life and live wholeheartedly for you. By your Holy Spirit please help me to spread the message of redemption through Jesus Christ to all who will listen. Amen.*

My thoughts, feelings and questions from the readings...

_____

_____

_____

_____

_____

_____

_____

_____

_____

_____

_____

_____

_____

_____

9

Exodus

Readings: Exodus 5-7, Psalm 31, 2 Corinthians 2

MOSES AND AARON GATHERED WITH the elders of the Israelites and shared with them the news that God was with them and had heard their cries. Moses performed miraculous signs and they believed (Ex. 4:30-31). With soft hearts their renewed trust led them to worship God (Ex. 4:31). However, it wasn't long before their hearts would doubt God's word as they witnessed the hardening of Pharaoh's heart. Pharaoh denied their request to leave Egypt (Ex. 5:1-2). He called the Israelites 'lazy' and increased their workload. The Israelites had become a stench to Pharaoh, he despised them, and the Israelites began to believe that they were not going to be rescued (Ex. 5:23).

Moses returned to God and asked why he had not rescued his people? Moses questioned why he had even been sent (Ex. 5:22-23). God reminded Moses that he had not forgotten and that he would come good on the promises made to Abraham. Yet the Israelites failed to listen because their suffering was too overwhelming (Ex. 6:9). God commanded Moses again to "Go, tell Pharaoh king of Egypt to let the Israelites go out of his country" (Ex. 6:10-11) and yet Moses doubted whether Pharaoh would listen and whether his 'faltering lips' would change Pharaoh's mind (Ex. 6:12).

But God encouraged him by saying that he will make him "like God to Pharaoh" and Aaron will be his prophet (Ex. 7:1). God will harden Pharaoh's heart so that his mighty acts of judgement can be displayed and so that even they will know that the Lord is God (Ex. 7:3-5). And just as he had said, great suffering was felt in Egypt as plagues were sent by God with Pharaoh unwilling to let them go.

Sin and suffering can either force us to throw ourselves upon the mercy of God or it deafens us to God's word. For Pharaoh it was in the great suffering of losing his own son that made him relent and let them leave. Even for Christians, suffering can often be paralysing, leading to complete distrust that God will ever hear our cries. The wailing on that final night in Egypt no doubt would have been distressing for all who could hear and yet, in the midst of terrible suffering, the Israelites finally began their journey home and God was with them (Ex. 12:41-42). God was always with them and when they were finally able to see all that God had done, they were able to place their trust in him (Ex. 14:31).

Prayer: Heavenly Father, thank you for being a refuge, a strong fortress. Thank you for rescuing and leading me into the way of peace. Father at times I feel like David as if I am broken pottery and yet you have not forgotten me. Please lead me, through your Holy Spirit, when the way forward is unclear, please keep my heart from becoming hardened and allow me to continue to forgive those who have hurt me as you have forgiven me so abundantly. Amen.

My thoughts, feelings and questions from the readings…

_____

_____

_____

_____

_____

_____

_____

_____

_____

_____

_____

_____

_____

_____

10

Free

Readings: Exodus 19-20, Psalm 19, Matthew 5

THE ENSLAVED NATION OF ISRAEL, now free, gathered at the base of Mt Sinai waiting for what was to come next. Moses was called up to the mountain to hear that they were not alone, that they were no longer lost, and that they were not without a home. God said to Moses "you yourselves have seen what I did to Egypt, and how I carried you on eagles' wings and brought you to myself. Now if you obey me fully and keep my covenant, then out of all nations you will be my treasured possession. Although the whole earth is mine, you will be for me a kingdom of priests and a holy nation" (Ex. 19:4-6).

This was a moment of great unity and fear amongst the people as they responded adamantly to Moses that they would do everything that God had said (Ex. 19:8). Only Moses was allowed to approach God on the mountain. The people were warned that they were not to 'force their way through to see the LORD' (Ex. 19:21), or the consequences of their disobedience would be disastrous. As God spoke to Moses, the people listened from a distance, to God's holy commands. Yahweh, was to be the only God that Israel worshipped.

They were not to exalt any object or person above or in place of God (Ex. 20:3-4). They were to remember the Sabbath day and set it apart as different from the others. They were not to steal life, possessions or relationships from others (Ex. 20:8-17). They were not to think that they could approach God without permission. Only God would choose who was to meet with him and how. This was the beginning of a pattern for how they were to live, no longer mistreated slaves by an owner who hated them, but a people loved by God, a kingdom with a King, with rules for living that were designed to preserve them, keep them safe and enable them to flourish as a nation.

In the New Testament, God himself in the form of a man, Jesus, sat on the mountain with his disciples and taught them about the goodness of the Law, that he was the only one who could fulfil its requirements (Matt. 5:17-18). The Law still promised to preserve God's people through obedience but it would not be through their own. It would only be through the obedience of Jesus.

Prayer: *Heavenly Father, thank you for the Law given to your people so long ago to demonstrate your holiness and expectations for perfection. Thank you that I no longer need to feel guilty for failing to keep your precious commandments. Thank you that I no longer need to strive for your approval by keeping the Law and feeling defeated by its impossibilities. Thank you that Jesus was able to keep your commands perfectly so that I might be credited with his righteousness. Please sanctify me through your Holy Spirit so that I might live a life pleasing to you. Amen.*

My thoughts, feelings and questions from the readings…

_____

_____

_____

_____

_____

_____

_____

_____

_____

_____

_____

_____

_____

_____

11

Atonement

Readings: *Exodus 25-26, John 19, Hebrews 9:11-28*
Dig Deeper: *Leviticus 16-17, Deuteronomy 12*

WITH THE LAW NOW ANNOUNCED to God's people, it was time for them to build God's dwelling place amongst them. The pattern for the tabernacle and its sanctuary for God to dwell in was to be made from materials that the people had offered from their hearts (Ex. 25:1). God would be meeting with Moses between the gold Cherubim that were guarding the covenant law to give all of his commandments to the Israelites (Ex. 25:22). His dwelling place was to be in accordance with the pattern set by himself, not by the Israelites. It was to be made just as Moses was shown on the mountain (Ex. 25:40, 26:30, 27:8). They were not to approach God on their own terms, only the High Priest who, at that moment in history, was Aaron (Lev. 16:3) and only on the day of atonement.

Once a year, atonement would be made for the sins of the Israelites (Lev. 16:34) and blood would be sprinkled on the atonement cover (Lev. 16:14). Aaron was to obey the prescribed pattern of animal sacrifice that God commanded. However, it wasn't long before the Israelites began establishing their own system of animal sacrifices based on the practices of the nations around them. They were offering sacrifices in whatever way they saw fit. But God loves order and purpose and he prescribed the *how* of animal sacrifices and the *why*. He warned them; "I will set my face against any Israelite or any foreigner residing among them who eats blood, and I will cut them off from the people. For the life of a creature is in the blood, and I have given it to you to make atonement for yourselves on the altar; it is the blood that makes atonement for one's life" (Lev. 17:10-11).

In the New Testament the apostle John mentions a unique detail of the crucifixion in his account. On the advice of the Jewish leaders, Pilate requested that the soldiers break the legs of those left on the crosses, this would quicken the process. But when they came to Jesus, they found that he was already dead, so, instead of breaking his legs, they pierced Jesus's side with a spear, bringing a sudden flow of blood and water (Jn. 19:31-34). John was adamant that this was the truth and he includes this information in his account to help sceptics believe - not only to prove that Jesus had died, but that the shedding of the blood fulfilled the commandment for the *how*. Jesus was the perfect sacrifice and his life blood was shed, taking on the curse for the world's sin and making the final atonement, once and for all. The world tries to make atonement through their works, establishing again their own sacrificial system but this should remind us that there really is only one way to approach a Holy God and that can only be through Jesus, God himself.

Prayer: Heavenly Father, thank you for sending your son Jesus to make the perfect atonement for my sin. Please help me to place my trust in Christ alone and not lean on my own understanding or ways of self-righteousness. Please help me to believe in your Son and his powerful work on the Cross and rest in the assurance that true forgiveness and reconciliation with you is offered to all who believe in Christ. Amen.

My thoughts, feelings and questions from the readings...

_____

_____

_____

_____

_____

_____

_____

_____

_____

_____

_____

_____

_____

12

Manna

Readings: Numbers 10-11, Psalm 78, John 6

WITH THE TABERNACLE COMPLETE AND the Law now spoken amongst the people, it was now the second year from the time they had left Egypt. The cloud had lifted as a sign to set out once again until resting in the Desert of Paran (Num. 10:11-12). With the tribe of Judah leading the others, they followed the ark of the covenant until it found them a place to rest (Num. 10:33). But the people complained about their afflictions and God was angry (Num. 11:1). They wailed and began to crave other food; they were tired of the manna God had provided them until now (Num. 11:4). They longed for meat and remembered the delicacies of Egypt that they had been given for free (Num. 11:5). They were no longer content with bread; they wanted more.

Moses felt the burden of the people and complained himself to God about his own affliction (Num. 11:14). Despite God's anger against them, he responded to Moses and the people by taking some of the power of the Spirit that God had given Moses to be distributed amongst seventy elders in order for the burden to be shared (Num. 11:25). Then

God drove quail in from the ocean and scattered them amongst the camp (Num. 11:31). There was more than enough food for all of them. God had given to them what they had asked for but their rebellion and distrust of God, by desiring to return to Egypt, did not come without judgement, for before they had even a chance to enjoy the meat, they were struck with a severe plague from God (Num. 11:33).

It's no coincidence that in the New Testament we discover that Jesus provided bread for the great crowd following him. He fed them with the intention of teaching them that they were to feed on him, he would satisfy them not only temporarily but eternally. He said to his disciples: "Do not work for food that spoils, but for food that endures to eternal life, which the Son of Man will give you" (Jn. 6:27). And the food that endures to eternal life is to simply believe in Jesus (Jn. 6:29). The Israelites failed to believe that God would sustain and provide for them. They lost sight of the promised land and all the delicacies that it would hold for them if only they could trust and wait. There have been countless times when I have acted just like the Israelites; I have complained before God, looked back to times of comfort and grown discontent with what God had given me. I am thankful for his continued mercy and faithfulness to his promises that he showed his people back then and to me now.

Prayer: *Heavenly Father, thank you that even though I fall short of your glory in so many ways, you sent Jesus, the true bread of life that gives life to the whole world. Thank you for enabling me to believe in him and feast on the satisfying richness of your word that gives life to weary souls. Please help me to long for spiritual food rather than just physical and help me turn from grumbling and complaining when life does not seem to go as planned. Please help me to persevere in times of suffering knowing that you are with me and have good things in store for me. Amen.*

My thoughts, feelings and questions from the readings...

13

Explore

Readings: Numbers 13-14, Psalm 34, 1 Corinthians 10

G OD SAID TO MOSES TO send out some men to explore the land that God was giving to Israel (Num. 13:1-2) - a leader was sent from each of the twelve tribes which included Joshua, from the tribe of Ephraim, and Caleb from the tribe of Judah. Moses asked them to report as to what the land was like, were the people strong or weak? Was the land good or bad? Were the towns protected or unprotected? What was the soil like? Were there trees? And, if possible, bring back some fruit of the land (Num. 13:18-20).

They explored the land for forty days and then they returned (Num. 13:25). They reported that the land did indeed flow with milk and honey, it was fruitful land! Yet the people who lived in the land were powerful and the cities fortified (Num. 13:27-28). When challenged by Caleb into taking possession of the land, they responded in fear that the people were stronger than they were and they spread this fear around the camp so that the Israelites would grow fearful also (Num. 13:30-32). The grumbling of the people began again and they longed to return to the safety of Egypt (Num. 14:3). Their fear would fail to lead them back to the comforts of Egypt and also forward into the promised land.

Ultimately fear drove them away from receiving the promises of God. They would live out their years in the wilderness with God's hand against them (Num. 14:32-35). The men whom God had sent to explore the land would die for their distrust. Only Joshua and Caleb, who believed in a God who is faithful to his promises, were saved that day (Num. 14:37-38). The apostle Paul, in the New Testament, spoke about Israel's history of rebellion against a loving God. He spoke about how their ancestors set their hearts on evil things (1 Cor. 10:1-6). He said they were written down to serve as a warning for those in the present age (1 Cor. 10:11). As Christians, they were tempted to think that they were superior to the Jews, that because of grace, their sins could not be held against them. Paul appealed to them to "flee from idolatry" (v14), to seek not just their own good but the good of others and to seek to live a holy life, giving glory to God in all that they did (v31).

There are many idols that plague my own life today; family, work, ministry, holidays, possessions, relationships. I have exalted many things above the Lord Jesus and indeed even beside him throughout my own history. Christians are not immune from the temptations that life offers but God is faithful. He forgives those who genuinely repent and place their trust in the Lord Jesus for salvation. He will provide a way out, a means to overcome temptations and trials that attempt to thwart his will for our lives.

Prayer: Heavenly Father, thank you that there is no temptation that is beyond your saving help. Thank you that even though I have failed many times to live a life that is pleasing to you, you continue to extend forgiveness. Please help me through your Holy Spirit to live a life that brings glory to you, that enables others to see Christ in me. Please help me to put no other god before you. Amen.

My thoughts, feelings and questions from the readings…

_____

_____

_____

_____

_____

_____

_____

_____

_____

_____

_____

_____

_____

_____

14

Rebel

Readings: Deuteronomy 1-4, Psalm 95, Hebrews 3

I
T WAS NOW FORTY YEARS since God had brought the Israelites out
of Egypt. The children who passed through the waters of the Red
Sea were now grown up and Moses was preparing the people once
again to enter the promised land. He was preparing their hearts
by expounding God's commandments to them in the wilderness (Deut.
1:1). Through all of their wanderings God had continued to bless the
people. He had chosen them despite their disobedience. He watched over
their journey ensuring that they lacked nothing (Deut. 2:7).

The Israelites' sin and rebellion against God had affected Moses also
and he would not be able to set foot in the promised land (Deut. 3:27).
It would be Joshua who would lead God's people across the Jordan and
inherit the land (Deut. 3:28). It was now time for Moses to commis-
sion Joshua, encourage and strengthen the people, and prepare the way
for a new generation with the hope that perhaps they may be faithful
to God's commandments. They were to observe them carefully and
through this they would show their "wisdom and understanding to the
nations" (Deut. 4:6). By knowing and understanding God's word they

would show that God is close to them, they would display a holy God and a holy people.

The writer of Hebrews urges its hearers to 'pay the most careful attention' to what has been heard so as not to drift away (Heb. 2:1). The message of the gospel is powerful; it is almost as if the writer of Hebrews is preparing hearts once again for his chosen ones to enter the land; God's resting place for those who would trust in his Son. He reminds them of their ancestors who hardened their hearts and would not listen to his voice, their hearts had gone astray (Heb. 3:8-10).

I am certainly prone to drifting. It can happen ever so slowly, yet over time it can feel as though I am alone and very far out from the shore. We can stay anchored to Christ by encouraging fellow believers daily, holding firmly to the message of Christ and fixing our thoughts on Jesus, the faithful one who is the master builder of God's house (Heb. 3:3).

Prayer: Heavenly Father, thank you that you have chosen me to share in the heavenly calling, for softening my heart so that I could hear your voice in the wilderness. Please help me to fix my thoughts on Jesus, to stay close to your word and to hold to my conviction in Jesus as the Messiah until my dying breath. Amen.

My thoughts, feelings and questions from the readings...

_____

_____

_____

_____

_____

_____

_____

_____

_____

_____

_____

_____

_____

15

Courage

Readings: Joshua 1-4, Psalm 37, Hebrews 4

WITH JOSHUA, NOW FULL OF the Spirit, the Israelites were ready to enter the land that God had promised to them long ago (Deut. 34:9). God was with Joshua, just like he was with Moses reminding them that he would never leave or forsake them (Josh. 1:5). God said to Joshua "Be strong and courageous, because you will lead these people to inherit the land I swore to their ancestors to give them" (Josh. 1:6). They would need strength and courage to confront their enemies but perhaps more importantly they were to be careful to obey 'all the law' that Moses had given them (Josh. 1:7).

The writer of Hebrews speaks about the promise of entering his rest which the land represented for the Israelites but now the promised land symbolises an eternal rest for all God's people. Just as Joshua urged the Israelites to be careful that they obey God, for Christians whose history is part of Joshua's, a similar warning remains for its readers to be 'careful that none of you be found to have fallen short of it' (Heb. 4:1). The writer of Hebrews has the benefit of understanding just how far the Israelites had fallen (Heb. 4:2).

It takes great courage to admit your weakness, to admit you failed. In fact, it takes great personal strength and vulnerability to admit that you are completely dependent on God. Yet that is what God asks of his people because he is faithful as the writer of Hebrews reminds us; we have a great high priest who has gone before us, that is Jesus the Son of God (Heb. 4:14). And this high priest is not like the ones from Israel's history. Though Jesus was tempted in every way, he never sinned, he was blameless (Heb. 4:15). Therefore today, God gives his people strength and courage to enter the land once again, his wonderful 'throne of grace', to find mercy and grace to help them in their every need. Just like God prepared the way for Israel to enter the land by defeating Israel's enemies, Jesus our High Priest has gone before us defeating our greatest enemies, sin and death, to enable us to enter into the 'rest' he promised long ago.

Prayer: *Heavenly Father, thank you for your mercy and grace that you have shown to me by providing your Son Jesus as the faithful High Priest who suffered in every way so as to show us that he understands all of our weaknesses. Please help me to cling to your word, which is alive and active. Please help me to bring my sin and failings to your throne of grace and not be fearful any longer. Please refresh my heart through your Holy Spirit and help me to serve with your Son's strength and courage. Amen.*

16

Saved

Readings: Joshua 5-6, Matthew 1, Hebrews 11

THE ISRAELITES HAD NOW STEPPED into the promised land. The second promise to Abraham was being fulfilled with the first of its cities to fall, Jericho. Before Joshua reached the famous city, he was met by a man who appeared to be part of an army. Joshua asked: "Are you for us or for our enemies?" (Josh. 5:13). Surprisingly, the man responded "Neither...but as commander of the army of the LORD I have now come" (v14). Joshua fell face down in preparation for a message from God reminiscent of a time when Moses was called by God (Josh. 5:15, Ex. 3:5).

They would need to listen carefully to God's instructions so that they would not bring about their own destruction (Josh. 6:18). For the next six days the Israelites were commanded by God to march around the fortified city and on the seventh day they were commanded to circle the city seven times (Josh. 6:15) with the priests sounding the trumpet blast (Josh. 6:16). They obeyed and the walls of Jericho fell down. That day the city was taken by the Israelites and every living thing destroyed

(Josh. 6:21), except for Rahab, the prostitute and her family, who had risked her life to hide the spies.

Rahab's entire household was saved that day because of the promises made to her family. She believed in the God of the Israelites before her city was destroyed. She had heard of his fame, she had acknowledged him as God in heaven above and on the earth below (Josh. 6:22-23, Deut. 4:39). She had trusted in a God that saves and shows no partiality. Rahab left her old life behind and married Salmon, the father of Boaz; the father of Obed, whose mother was Ruth; Obed the father of Jesse; and Jesse the father of King David (Matt. 1:5-6). Rahab was grafted into the tribe of Judah, the same tribe that led the Israelites into the promised land.

It would not be for another 1400 years until the last Saviour would lead his people into the eternal promised land. Rahab was commended by the author of Hebrews as someone who lived by faith. She had placed her confidence in a God whom she had not seen but had only heard of. She was a foreigner; the city of Jericho was no longer hers. She was now walking with a people who were looking forward to a heavenly city and a place to call home.

Prayer: Heavenly Father, thank you for leading me into the promised land, a place of rest where I can place my confidence in a God that saves his people, that leads them, that teaches them. Thank you for saving Rahab and her family that day, and for being faithful to your promises that a Saviour would come from the line of Judah. Thank you for the Messiah, Jesus, who lived by faith perfectly and gave us the strength and courage to trust in his work and not our own. Please help me to continue to walk by faith knowing that your word is true and trustworthy. Amen.

My thoughts, feelings and questions from the readings…

_____

_____

_____

_____

_____

_____

_____

_____

_____

_____

_____

_____

_____

17

Serve

Readings: Joshua 23-24, Ezekiel 20, Ephesians 5-6

ALONG TIME HAD NOW PASSED, the Israelites were living in the promised land and God had given them rest from their enemies (Josh. 23:1). Joshua was very old now and he gathered the people together and reminded them that their God fought for them. There was still more fighting to be done but Joshua commanded them to be very strong and careful to obey the Law. They were not to associate with the nations that remained amongst them and they were not to serve or bow down to their gods (Josh. 23:7). They were to cling to God and be very careful to love him (Josh. 23:11).

If they turned away and became friends with the nations or intermarried with them, they would perish in the land. God would no longer drive out the nations, instead they would become snares for the Israelites (Josh. 23:12-13). Joshua gave them a great warning but he also reminded them of the wonderful promises of God that they had been given. They gathered together and recommitted their lives to serving God alone (Josh. 24:24). This was a wonderful picture of renewed hope amongst the Israelites, a new resolve to serve God wholeheartedly.

The prophet Ezekiel, 800 years later, painted a very different picture of what happened next in the promised land. They were not careful in obeying the Law. When they saw any 'high hill or any leafy tree, there they offered their sacrifices, and made offerings that aroused God's anger' (Ezek. 20:28). They wanted to be like the nations, they sacrificed their own children in the fire and served idols made from 'wood and stone' (Ezek. 20:32). Even though God's children rebelled, like a good father, God disciplined his children for a time but for the sake of his holy name, he gathered his rebellious children and brought them home (Ezek. 20:41).

When the apostle Paul wrote to the Christians living in Ephesus, they were surrounded by a culture that worshipped idols. In fact, this was a church of both Jewish and Gentile converts. How difficult to leave a culture that was your identity for most of your life and then grasp hold of a new identity in Christ. Paul urged them to live a life of love which imitated the costly love of Christ (Eph. 5:2) and to live like people of the light (v8).

Prayer: Heavenly Father, thank you for bringing me out of the darkness and into your glorious light. I confess there is still so much sin holding me back from serving and loving you alone. Please help me to put away the deeds done in the darkness and help me to make the most of every opportunity to serve you in wholeness, that I might live a life pleasing to you in every way. Amen.

My thoughts, feelings and questions from the readings...

_____

_____

_____

_____

_____

_____

_____

_____

_____

_____

_____

_____

_____

18

Renew

Readings: Ruth 1-4, Isaiah 40, Luke 1-3

I N THE TIME OF THE Judges in Israel there was a famine in the promised land and a family living in Bethlehem left their home to live in Moab (Ruth 1:1). The people of Moab had been intertwined with Jewish history from the beginning and it had long been a place of immorality and temptation for the Israelites (Gen. 19:37). One cannot help but think that this decision to move could have tragic consequences for this Jewish family. As predicted they did not find rest in Moab. In fact, it wasn't long before the head of the family died followed by his two sons, leaving his wife a widow in a foreign land (Ruth 1:5).

Her name was Naomi and before her sons had died, they had married Moabite women, Orpah and Ruth (Ruth 1:4). Ruth's very name means 'friend' and she was indeed a great friend to Naomi. After losing everything, the pair travelled back to Naomi's home, the land of Judah (Ruth 1:6). There was a beautiful moment where Naomi released Ruth from the obligation to leave her own home land. Weeping aloud, Ruth clung to Naomi and said "don't urge me to leave you or to turn back from you. Where you go, I will go, and where you stay, I will stay. Your people will be my people and your God my God" (Ruth 1:16). Like Rahab (Josh. 2), Ruth was committing herself and her future to following the God of Israel.

On the return trip home Naomi became terribly depressed to the point of wanting to change her name to 'Mara', claiming that God had made her life very bitter (Ruth 1:20). Ruth believed that her suffering had come from God. When trials come, we might be tempted to think that God is punishing us or holding out on us and yet in every moment of our lives God is actively working for our good and his glory, in order to bring us back to him when we have wandered.

As time passed, Ruth the foreigner, met Boaz and because he was closely related to Naomi, he was able to redeem her land and preserve the family name. He married Ruth and became for her a Kinsman Redeemer and God blessed her through a son, named Obed. Naomi's fortunes were restored, she gained not only a son but a grandson too. This grandson was later to be named in the genealogy of Jesus, the Messiah, along with his mother, a foreigner (Ruth 4:18-22, Lk. 3:32). Who could have imagined the outcome of this series of events? And yet God was in control the entire time, working out his salvation purposes - for this family and for humanity.

Prayer: Heavenly Father, thank you that even when life appears to be out of control, you are in control. Thank you that you have my life in your hands and that you are working out all things for my good and for your purposes. Please help me to trust you more in these times and lean on your understanding, renew my life and sustain me through the Holy Spirit. Amen.

My thoughts, feelings and questions from the readings...

_____

_____

_____

_____

_____

_____

_____

_____

_____

_____

_____

_____

_____

19

Kingdom

Readings:1 Samuel 8-10, Isaiah 55, Acts 13

THE ISRAELITES GREW DISCONTENT ONCE again and craved the kingdoms that the surrounding nations had; they desired a king (1 Sam. 8:5). They had rejected God as their king long ago (1 Sam. 8:8). God told the prophet Samuel to warn them of the consequences of gaining an earthly king: the king they choose will take from them rather than give; he will take their sons and their daughters; the best of their fields, their servants, their animals and ultimately themselves. They will be enslaved all over again (1 Sam. 8:17).

Despite God's warnings, they refused to listen and continued to desire to be like the other nations with a king who would lead them into battle and fight for them (1 Sam. 8:20). It seemed Israel had forgotten again what God had been doing for them from the very beginning. Despite already knowing that his own children's decisions would lead to disastrous consequences, he gave them what they wanted and Saul was anointed as the first king of Israel (1 Sam. 10:1). Saul reigned for another forty years (Acts 13:21) until his death sparked a battle for the throne that ultimately divided the nation of Israel. But now the stage had been set for God's chosen king, a man after his own heart, David, son of Jesse. His family line would continue to rule forever; the beginning of God's final promise to Abraham in which his offspring would bring blessing to all the nations (2 Sam. 7:12).

During Paul's first missionary journey, he visited Pisidian Antioch in modern-day Turkey and sat down with both Jews and Gentiles in the local synagogue. After reading from the Law and the Prophets, the leaders of the synagogue asked for a 'word of exhortation' (Acts 13:15). The Greek word for this is *paraklesis* which means to encourage, to urge, to console, to bring comfort and to appeal. Paul took this wonderful opportunity to preach the gospel, explaining to them that Jesus was the promised Saviour for Israel (Acts 13:23), that their sins were forgiven and that "through him everyone who believes is set free from every sin" (Acts 13:39). The gospel message indeed brings comfort to the lost and yet it also brings persecution for the faithful. Despite the hatred and jealousy that the disciples were experiencing during this time in history they were filled with joy (Acts 13:52). Unlike the worldly pursuit of happiness, Christian joy is a wonderful gift given by God, through the Holy Spirit. It is a deep feeling of inner delight knowing the certainty of salvation from judgement, forgiveness of sins and the hope of eternal life through Christ.

Prayer: Heavenly Father, thank you that your wonderful message of salvation extends to all nations, both Jews and Gentiles which includes me. Thank you for appointing me to eternal life and giving me the faith to believe in your powerful message. Thank you for Jesus who through him, I can be forgiven for all my sins and failings and be given the gift of the Holy Spirit. Please cultivate a deep joy within me through your Holy Spirit that can overcome any earthly trial. Amen.

My thoughts, feelings and questions from the readings...

_____

_____

_____

_____

_____

_____

_____

_____

_____

_____

_____

_____

_____

20

Fountain

Readings:1 Samuel 15-17, Psalm 36, Romans 2-3

AVID'S RISE TO KINGSHIP WAS not without suffering. Pursued relentlessly by Saul, he was all too aware of the sinfulness of man, he saw it in those around him and he saw it in his own heart. He observed the utter depravity of man, people who were unable to "detect or hate their sin" (Ps. 36:2). David compared humanity's unfaithfulness to the faithfulness of God. He spoke of the height and breadth of God's love and faithfulness, righteousness and justice (Ps. 36:5-6). He referred to the abundant provision of life, he said "for with you is the fountain of life; in your light we see light" (Ps. 36:9). David understood that we're unable to see the goodness of God until we're called out of darkness and into the light.

The apostle Paul counted himself as among the wicked, the unrighteous and unfaithful. He was unable to detect how fallen he was until he was literally blinded by the light of Jesus. In his letter to the Romans, he spoke of the wickedness of mankind. He, too, observed that there was no one righteous (Rom. 3:10-11). The power of sin blinds people and yet there is good news. David spoke of this good news, this fountain of life and Paul showed us what that good news was "for all have sinned and fall short of the glory of God, and *all* are justified freely by his grace through the redemption that came by Christ Jesus" (Rom. 3:23-24). Both David and Paul understood the depth of God's love and mercy and they both prayed that God would help his people to stand firm in the promises of God even while surrounded by darkness.

David's thoughts have shaped Paul's theology as he expressed what David knew long ago but which now had been fulfilled through a risen Christ, he says "for I am convinced that neither death nor life, neither angels nor demons, neither the present nor the future, nor any powers, neither height nor depth, nor anything else in all creation, will be able to separate us from the love of God that is in Christ Jesus our Lord" (Rom. 8:38-39). How wonderful it is that even when we are pursued by enemies, surrounded in darkness or feeling deeply alone, God is with us.

Prayer: Heavenly Father, thank you that nothing can separate me from your love. Thank you for allowing me to see the depth of my sin in order to understand the depth of your mercy and grace. Please help me to stand firm in your promises and the knowledge that I am forever safe in your care. Please continue to extend your mercy and grace to your chosen people that they may know the true light of life. Amen.

My thoughts, feelings and questions from the readings…

_____

_____

_____

_____

_____

_____

_____

_____

_____

_____

_____

_____

_____

_____

_____

_____

21

Unfailing

Readings: 1 Samuel 22-25, Psalm 143, Matthew 26

WHEN DAVID WAS IN THE wilderness he experienced times, both physically and spiritually hiding from his enemies, yet continuing to find strength in God. David himself, became a refuge for those who were being pursued, those in distress, those in debt and the discontent (1 Sam. 22:2). In Psalm 143, David's thoughts are written down as if they were being poured out as he cried out to God for mercy and relief (Ps. 143:1). Pursued by his enemies, feeling crushed and in despair, he was aware that he was surrounded by darkness, his spirit growing faint and his heart dismayed (vv3-4).

David appeared to feel quite distant from God, perhaps feeling alone and yet he remembered all that God had done in the past (v5). He longed for spiritual water and to be close to God again (v6). David was overwhelmed, he longed to be comforted and encouraged by God; he longed to know the way he should go, he entrusted his life to God (vv7-8). He prayed to be rescued as he hid himself in the LORD, he said "Teach me to do your will, for you are my God, may your good

Spirit lead me on level ground" (v10). In times of intense hardship and suffering it is easy to feel as though God is distant, like life is somehow out of control. But David teaches us how to respond in these moments. He pleaded, he cried, he thirsted, he remembered and he entrusted his life again to God. David was clinging to the promises of God through a very dry spiritual season, a time of great testing.

In the gospel of Matthew an account is given of the night before Jesus died. Jesus went to a place called Gethsemane with his disciples. He was distressed and he said to Peter and the two sons of Zebedee "my soul is overwhelmed with sorrow to the point of death. Stay here and keep watch with me" (Matt. 26:36-38). Then he fell down with his face to the ground and prayed to his Father "My Father, if it is possible, may this cup be taken from me. Yet not as I will, but as you will" (v39). Like David, Jesus models a response for us when we are feeling overwhelmed with sorrow; he prays, he prays and he prays again pleading for the Father to take away the sorrow and yet at the same time trusting that God's answer is always in accordance with his will and is always perfect. Jesus highlights the importance of being on guard in these great times of testing in our life. Do not fall asleep, keep praying and watching, keep pleading and trusting because God always keeps his promises and his timing is perfect.

Prayer: *Heavenly Father, please help me cling to the promise that you will never leave me or forsake me during seasons of deep loneliness and suffering. Thank you that Jesus willingly entrusted his life to you so that I may have life in his name. Please lead me and teach me to do your will for you are my God and I trust in you. Amen.*

My thoughts, feelings and questions from the readings...

_____

_____

_____

_____

_____

_____

_____

_____

_____

_____

_____

_____

_____

_____

_____

_____

22

Home

Readings: 2 Samuel 5-7, Psalm 89, Luke 7

WHEN DAVID BECAME KING, HE was thirty years old and reigned for forty years (2 Sam. 5:4). He captured the 'fortress of Zion', the city of David (2 Sam. 5:7), despite the Jebusites' taunts that he wouldn't be able to get past the 'blind and the lame' (2 Sam. 5:6). This was now David's home and because the LORD was with him, he grew more and more powerful (2 Sam. 5:9-10). A palace was built that the 'blind and lame' could not enter (2 Sam. 5:8) and David knew that God had 'established him as king over Israel and had exalted his kingdom for the sake of his people Israel' (2 Sam. 5:12).

David brought the ark home with celebration and dancing much to the disdain of his first wife and Saul's daughter Michal (2 Sam. 6:20). His love for God and his commands were evident and he responded to Michal's jealousy by affirming his utter devotion to God (2 Sam. 6:22). Moved to give God a proper home and a house for the ark of God, David consulted the prophet Nathan but God stopped him and said that it would not be he, David, who established a house, but it would be God himself (2 Sam. 7:11b). God affirmed his promises to David that he would raise up one from David's offspring to succeed him and he would establish his kingdom (2 Sam. 7:12), "your house and your kingdom will endure forever before me and your throne will be established forever" (2 Sam. 7:16). With this news David was driven to prayer; acknowledging the sovereignty of God and his mere humanness (2 Sam. 7:18-19), he praised God for his greatness and his mighty acts of redemption for Israel (2 Sam. 7:23). He pleaded with God to keep his promise for the sake of his name and asked that he might bless the house of David forever (2 Sam. 7:29).

In Luke's gospel we see the same humility that David possessed before God in the heart of a centurion. Whilst the 'elders of the Jews' pleaded with Jesus to heal the centurion's servant based on the work that he had done in building the synagogue (Lk. 7:4-6), Jesus didn't heal the servant based on their pleas, he healed the servant by grace. (Lk. 7:6-8). Both stories teach us that as humans we are undeserving of God's kindness. There is no amount of justification that can make him help us. Like the lame and the blind who were enemies of David, we are the real enemies. Jesus was and is greater. He was preparing a people for his true power and greatness as he was heading closer to home. The prophet Nathan's words were about to be fulfilled in their very presence "I will punish him with a rod wielded by men, with floggings inflicted by human hands" (2 Sam. 7:14b). The City of David would once again become a place of weeping, jealousy and celebration.

Prayer: Heavenly Father, thank you for the promise you made to David so long ago that has now been fulfilled in Jesus. I am undeserving of the love and kindness that you have shown to me. Thank you for electing me to life and showing me the true greatness of your Son. Thank you for coming to my home and healing me so that I might live forever in your Heavenly home with you. Amen.

My thoughts, feelings and questions from the readings...

_____

_____

_____

_____

_____

_____

_____

_____

_____

_____

_____

_____

23

Broken

Readings: 2 Samuel 11-12, Psalm 51, 1 John 1-3

AVID CONQUERED MANY CITIES AND armies in his time as king but perhaps his most infamous battle was his quest to have Bathsheba. First seeing her bathing on a rooftop, he slept with her and then conspired to have her husband Uriah killed in battle (2 Sam. 11:14-15). David sinned greatly before God and judgement was felt in the loss of David and Bathsheba's first son (2 Sam. 12:18). Despite David's pleas and fasting, God did not relent in his decision. Accepting God's judgement, he comforted Bathsheba and they conceived another son. They named him Solomon (2 Sam. 12:24).

David experienced severe grief during this time. He was broken because of sin and pleaded that God would forgive him (Ps. 51:7). God heard his pleas and graciously acted. God blessed him with a son who was loved by God and would grow up to be the next king of Israel. Despite David's unfaithfulness, God remained faithful to his promises. David was a sinner just like us. He knew he could not have fellowship with God if his sin remained unconfessed. For Christian believers, we too can have fellowship with God "if we confess our sins, he is faithful and just and will forgive us our sins and purify us from all unrighteousness" (1 Jn. 1:9). David's sin began with the "lust of the flesh, the lust of the eyes, and the pride of life"; he thought he could have anything he wanted. But this type of attitude does not come from God but from the world (1 Jn. 2:16).

David feared that God would cast him from his presence, that he would take away the Holy Spirit from him (Ps. 51:11). For Christian believers we do not need to fear this. God promises eternal life; he promises the Holy Spirit (1 Jn. 2:27), though we are exhorted to 'remain in him' (Jn. 15:4). David showed us that even a man chosen after God's own heart was capable of messing things up, but God heard his confession and restored him. This is a wonderful hope as we continue to stumble and fall as mere humans knowing that God will never take his Holy Spirit from us.

Prayer: Heavenly Father, thank you that you love me; that you have blessed me with children. Thank you that despite my pride at times and lustful looks at things of the world, you have forgiven me through the atoning sacrifice of your Son, and not just my sins but for the whole world. Please help me to walk in the light and to confess my sins when your Holy Spirit convicts me. Please help me to forgive others quickly and to love them as you have loved me. Amen.

My thoughts, feelings and questions from the readings...

_____

_____

_____

_____

_____

_____

_____

_____

_____

_____

_____

_____

_____

24

Wisdom

Readings: 1 Kings 2-9, Proverbs 14, 1 Corinthians 1

THE CITY OF DAVID BECAME David's final resting place and the throne was given to his son Solomon (1 Kings 2:10-12). Solomon would reign for another forty years until he too would find his resting place in Jerusalem (1 Kings 11:42-43). King Solomon was 'greater in riches and wisdom than all the other kings of the earth. His fame had spread throughout the whole ancient world who sought audience with Solomon to hear the wisdom God had put in his heart' (1 Kings 10:23-24). Amongst Solomon's achievements was the building of the temple and the royal palace (1 Kings 9:10). But Solomon had made unwise choices for his wives. He had married Pharaoh's daughter and aligned himself with the nation of Egypt. He enslaved the inhabitants still living in the land from the 'Amorites, Hittites, Perizzites, Hivites and Jebusites' and forced them to build the temple and his royal palace (1 Kings 9:20-21).

Solomon's wisdom turned to folly as his wives increased and became a snare for his very heart. The very people he enslaved turned his affections to their gods and he forsook his devotion to God (1 Kings 11:4).

Despite God appearing to Solomon twice and warning him to keep his commands and walk faithfully with him, Solomon's disobedience resulted in the division of an entire kingdom. Only one tribe remained 'for the sake of David' and for Jerusalem - the tribe of Judah (1 Kings 11:12-13). From Rehoboam (Solomon's son) to King Ahaz, the kings of Israel 'did evil in the eyes of the Lord'. Nevertheless, for the sake of his servant David, God was not willing to destroy Judah. He was committed to the promise he had made to David and his descendants (2 Kings 8:18-19). The people of Israel, his chosen ones, were shrouded in darkness. Like their worthless idols, they too had become worthless (2 Kings 17:15).

In Paul's time God's people were again surrounded by the nations; They lived in the midst of the wisdom of the age - 'philosophy'; and were at risk of placing their trust in human wisdom and creating a syncretistic version of Christianity which was no longer centred on the power of the crucified Christ. The 'message of the cross is foolishness to those who are perishing, but to us who are being saved it is the power of God' (1 Cor. 1:18). God chose weak kings; he chose despised things; he chose us not for our faithfulness but to prove his covenantal faithfulness. He is trustworthy and his word is good and truly does endure forever.

Prayer: Heavenly Father, thank you for your enduring love and faithfulness to your servant David and his descendants. Thank you that we inherit the promises you made to them through trusting in Jesus Christ. Thank you for reminding me that your power and wisdom is revealed through the weak and despised things of this world. Please help me through your Holy Spirit to boast in him alone. Amen.

25

Beneath

Readings: Jonah 1-4, Psalm 40, Matthew 8

URING THE REIGN OF JOASH, King of Judah, Jeroboam, son of Jehoash, became King in Samaria (2 Kings 14:23). This was the time Jonah was a prophet of the northern kingdom of Israel around the 8th Century BC (2 Kings 14:25). Recognised as a prophet in Islam with his story included in the Quran, his father's name Amittai means 'my truth'. Children and adults alike love the story of Jonah. A great whale is imagined in the story and Jonah sitting in its belly wondering what will happen next. But the story of Jonah is truly remarkable because it communicates deeply about *who* God is.

When Jonah was asked by God to go to Nineveh to preach, he ignored the call and instead headed for Tarshish (Jnh. 1:3), his motive being 'to flee from the LORD'; and God reminded him, through a "violent storm", that he could not hide from God or flee from him and that he was indeed God of the land and God of the sea. Interestingly, during the whole adventure, there was never an outward sign that Jonah was afraid. He slept while sailors ran frantically around him pleading with him to wake up (Jnh. 1:6). He acknowledged his responsibility and surrendered his life in saving his companions.

God's provision was on wondrous display as he provided a huge fish to swallow Jonah and he remained in the belly for three days and three nights. It was inside the fish that we learnt of Jonah's inner thoughts and the turmoil of his soul as he came before God in prayer. He spoke of his distress and cried for help as he sank into the depths of the sea. When life was ebbing away from Jonah he remembered his God and prayed. He remembered God's wonderful mercy in bringing him up from the pit. Indeed, even in the belly of a great fish Jonah was content and satisfied and felt as if he had already been saved (Jnh. 2:9).

It is no coincidence that a similar story presents itself in the New Testament. As Jesus and his companions travelled by boat a furious storm came up on the lake and the waves broke over the boat while the disciples frantically attempted to wake up Jesus pleading with him to "save us, we're going to drown" (Matt. 8:25). Instead of joining in on their fear, he got up and told the wind and waves to stop and it was completely calm (v 26). At that moment he was teaching them that he is the "God of heaven, who made the sea and the dry land" (Jnh. 1:9). Ultimately the story of Jonah points to the complete rebellion of mankind, but in keeping with God's merciful nature, Jonah and his companions were saved by grace that day. Unlike Jonah, who was completely guilty of his sin, Jesus willingly offered his sinless life to save others. He willingly hurled himself into the deep so that he could achieve salvation for us once and for all.

Prayer: *Heavenly Father, Creator and Lord of the Heavens and the Earth. Thank you that even though like Jonah I completely rebelled against your will for my life you rescued me from the darkness. Thank you that you heard my prayers, and listened to my cry for help when I felt my life was ebbing away. Thank you for your mercy and grace through Jesus. Please help me to proclaim your gospel to others that they might be saved too. Amen.*

My thoughts, feelings and questions from the readings...

_____

_____

_____

_____

_____

_____

_____

_____

_____

_____

_____

_____

_____

26

Restored

Readings: 2 Kings 16-19, Isaiah 38, 1 Corinthians 2

LIGHT WAS BEGINNING TO DAWN for the people of God. King Hezekiah led an extraordinary life under intense pressure. His dad Ahaz was a terrible father who sacrificed Hezekiah's own brother and engaged in detestable practices whilst he was King of Judah (2 Kings 16:3). It seemed though, that despite the unfaithfulness of his father, this did not deter him from his own faithfulness and for a time it seemed as if Hezekiah could just be the one to save Israel. He removed the high places, smashed the sacred stones and cut down the Asherah poles. He trusted in Yahweh, the God of Israel. Indeed, the writer of 2 Kings says that "there was no one like him among all the kings of Judah, either before him or after him" (2 Kings 18:5). He kept the commands and held fast to God and never stopped following him and God was with him (2 Kings 18:6-7).

Hezekiah's name means "Yahweh strengthens" and it seemed in his early life that his faith went from strength to strength. Following the surrender of the Northern Kingdom to the Assyrians, Jerusalem came under threat and Sennacherib sent a delegate to persuade the surviving remnant to turn their confidence from God and instead place their trust in the King of Assyria, a human foreign king. In response, Hezekiah tore his clothes and went to the temple and waited for word. He prayed for deliverance so that God's name would be known throughout the earth(2 Kings 19:19). God heard Hezekiah and promised to save a remnant and out of Mount Zion (2 Kings 19:3-31). That night, while everyone was sleeping, the angel of God put to death a hundred and eighty-five thousand men in the Assyrian camp. Sennacherib retreated and was killed by his very own sons (2 Kings 19:35-37).

One might assume that it was Hezekiah's faithfulness that saved Judah that day, that caused the remnant to survive, but God made a strong point that it was the "zeal of the LORD almighty" that accomplished the victory that day (2 Kings 19:31). That same zeal would ensure a King would reign on David's throne forever (Isa. 9:7). Hezekiah was a shadow of what was to come. Like the kings before him, he would die too. The one true king was coming to restore all things and provide life everlasting for all who place their trust and confidence in him alone.

Prayer: *Heavenly Father, thank you that you are utterly committed to your people. Thank you that you are always working, always faithful and always keep your promises. Thank you for saving a remnant that bore Jesus, the Messiah. Thank you for restoring me and giving me life everlasting in his name. Amen.*

My thoughts, feelings and questions from the readings...

_____

_____

_____

_____

_____

_____

_____

_____

_____

_____

_____

_____

_____

_____

27

Bones

Readings: 2 Kings 20-25, Ezekiel 37, Acts 1-2

FOLLOWING THE DEATH OF HEZEKIAH, his son Manasseh succeeded him (2 Kings 20:21) and rebuilt everything his father had destroyed. It seemed that judgement was coming for God's people who had again turned their backs on him. During the reign of Zedekiah, Judah was finally taken into captivity, away from their home and the temple destroyed (2 Kings 25:21). However, God had warned the Israelites long before, that judgement was coming. He longed for them to turn back to him. It was on the banks of the Kebar River in the land of the Babylonians that God spoke to Ezekiel, a priest exiled from Jerusalem after the reign of Josiah, a king who tried hard to reform the people (Ezek. 1:1-2).

Ezekiel was called by God to speak his word to the exiles, whether they would listen or not; he was commanded to speak the truth (Ezek. 2:7). And the truth was truly difficult to hear. Imagine being told you are "obstinate and stubborn", "rebellious", "hardened", "wicked", "evil", "vile" and "adulterous" (Ezek. 2:1-5). The temple that they thought contained their God was about to be destroyed and God was departing; he was leaving them (Ezek. 10:18). The exiles were truly alone; God's judgement had come; all hope was lost. Or was it? Thankfully God never depended on the Israelites being faithful to his Covenant. From the very beginning humans were unfaithful and yet he promised, from the very beginning, to bring his people back to him. So if the story ended there then God was not and is not who he says he is.

God renewed his promise through Ezekiel, saying "I will gather you from the nations and bring you back from the countries where you have been scattered and I will give you back the land of Israel again" (Ezek. 11:17). The people will return and turn from their idolatry. He said "I will give them an undivided heart and put a new spirit in them; I will remove from them their heart of stone and give them a heart of flesh" (Ezek. 11:19). A time is coming when God's people will cross from death to life, from dry lifeless bones, to a new body filled with the breath of God, filled with God's life-giving Spirit (Ezek. 37:11-14). On that day, God's servant David (the Messiah) will be king over them, and they will have one shepherd, God said "I will make a covenant of peace with them; it will be an everlasting covenant. I will establish them and increase their numbers, and I will put my sanctuary among them forever. My dwelling-place will be with them; I will be their God, and they will be my people" (Ezek. 37:26-27). What a wonderful hope to cling to in what would have been a lonely, desperate time for the exiles. How mightily they would have wept by the rivers of Babylon for all that was lost and yet God would find them again and bring them home.

Prayer: Heavenly Father, I know that without your son Jesus standing between you and me, I am just like the lost exiles, utterly sinful and unfaithful, unable to keep your commandments. Thank you for renewing your covenant and grafting me into Abraham's family through Jesus. Thank you for your Holy Spirit that breathes life into my whole being and enables me to see your goodness and faithfulness and turn back and trust Jesus. Amen.

My thoughts, feelings and questions from the readings...

_____

_____

_____

_____

_____

_____

_____

_____

_____

_____

_____

_____

_____

_____

28

Rebuild

FTER SEVENTY YEARS IN EXILE, as God had promised, he
appointed Cyrus, a foreign king to bring his people home. A
proclamation was made by Cyrus king of Persia whose heart
God had moved to enable the exiled to prepare and return
to Jerusalem to rebuild the temple (Ezra 1:3). Thousands of exiled Jews,
whose hearts God had moved, returned home (Ezra 2:64). This was a
beautiful moment where the people of God gathered to sing praises to
God celebrating the foundation that had been laid; they sang out "He
is good; his love toward Israel endures forever" (Ezra 3:11). As an on-
looker all that you may have heard that day was celebrating, yet among
those rejoicing, were also those who wept, those who remembered the
beauty and glory of the old temple which would never compare to the
new (Ezra 3:12).

There were more tears to come as Ezra learned that despite the
temple being rebuilt and the joy the people had in returning home, they
had not remained separate from the nations around them. They had
intermarried and continued in their rejection of God's holy laws (Ezra

9). In learning this, Ezra fell to his knees, hands spread out to God and he prayed "I am too ashamed and disgraced, my God, to lift up my face to you, because our sins are higher than our heads and our guilt has reached to the heavens…" (Ezra 9:6). Whilst Ezra acknowledged the new life God had given them and the remnant God had preserved for the sake of his covenantal faithfulness, he still deeply feared that they would be cut off forever because of their unfaithfulness (Ezra 9:15). In witnessing Ezra's prayers and confession, the Israelites wept bitterly, all too aware of the depth of their sin.

It is often distressing and troubling when we become aware of our own failings. We might look to others in the faith and wonder "will I ever be as faithful as they are?" We become aware of our failures even more sometimes, knowing that there is still a lot of work to be done in us. When the apostle Peter spoke to the onlookers who were marvelling at the healing he had just performed, he spoke a powerful message to us also: "Repent, then, and turn to God, so that your sins may be wiped out, that times of refreshing may come from the Lord, and that he may send the Messiah, who has been appointed for you - even Jesus" (Acts 3:19-20). I long for those times of refreshment, of knowing God's goodness and that his love surely does endure forever. But they only come through repentance and that can often be a painful process.

Prayer: *Heavenly Father, thank you that you love us, that you long for us to be sanctified and made holy. Father thank you that we are forgiven when we come to you in confession. Please help me to walk in that truth and rejoice at the new life you have given through Jesus, the foundation of my faith. Amen.*

My thoughts, feelings and questions from the readings…

_____

_____

_____

_____

_____

_____

_____

_____

_____

_____

_____

_____

_____

_____

29

Wait

Readings: Micah 4-5, Isaiah 49, Luke 1-2

F
OR FOUR HUNDRED YEARS GOD's people lived in darkness, enslaved again by foreign kings, reminiscent of their time in Egypt. They had not heard from God since the final words of the Prophet Malachi and were now waiting for the promised Messiah. In the midst of the silence and the pervading reign of the Romans, a Saviour was coming from Bethlehem to rescue them (Mic. 5:2); a Saviour that would have compassion on them and would guide them and lead them beside springs of water (Isa. 49:10). A Saviour that was coming not only to save, but also to judge and those who would place their hope in him would not be disappointed (Isa. 49:23).

Redemption was coming for Israel (Isa. 49:26). The time for God's promises to Abraham to be fulfilled was coming and John had been chosen to 'make ready a people prepared for the Lord', filled with the Holy Spirit even before he was born (Lk 1:15-17). His father Zechariah, a priest whose ancestry can be traced back to Aaron through Abijah (Lk. 1:5, 1 Chron. 24:7-19), was filled with joy as he proclaimed that the Messiah, the 'horn of salvation' (Lk. 1:69) was coming to 'shine on those living in darkness' (Lk. 1:79). Following the birth of John, several months later a child was born in Bethlehem whose parents had travelled from Nazareth (Lk. 2:4). His name was Jesus and he belonged to the house and line of David (Lk. 2:4).

Both John and Jesus grew in strength and wisdom and God was with them (Lk. 1:80, 2:52). The parallels in these stories between Aaron and Moses and John and Jesus are uncanny and they each play a pivotal role in preparing a nation for redemption. In each of these stories God used the pervading darkness to make way for the light. It is truly wonderful that we have been given this rich history of the unfolding story of God's promises through the Bible so that we can truly understand the depth and beauty of God's grace in sending his only son into the world to save us.

Prayer: *Heavenly Father, thank you that you did not leave your people in darkness; that you sent John first into the world to make way for your Son, to set the stage for his quiet but timely arrival. Thank you for the Scriptures that provide us with the rich history of how you have worked through your own people and your enemies to bring about the fulfilment of your glorious promises. Amen.*

My thoughts, feelings and questions from the readings...

_____

_____

_____

_____

_____

_____

_____

_____

_____

_____

_____

_____

_____

_____

_____

_____

_____

30

Pleased

Readings: Luke 3-5, Isaiah 61, Acts 5-6

N O LONGER A CHILD, THE time had come for Jesus's public ministry to begin. The word of God came to John 'in the wilderness' and he travelled throughout 'Jordan preaching a baptism of repentance for the forgiveness of sins' (Lk.3:2-3). This was to fulfil the prophet Isaiah's message that a voice from the wilderness would come to prepare the way for the Messiah (Lk. 3:4). The people waited with anticipation thinking in their hearts "could this be the Messiah?" (Lk. 3:15). But John did not leave them in anticipation for long as he exhorted that "one who is more powerful than I will come, the straps of whose sandals I am not worthy to untie" (Lk. 3:16).

Baptised in the Jordan by John, Jesus, now thirty, was commissioned by the Holy Spirit for ministry (Lk. 3:22-23). Now in the power of the Spirit he was led into the wilderness for forty days of testing and then returned home to declare the words of Isaiah in the synagogue where he spent his time as a youth (Lk. 4:17-19). Knowing they would reject him as the Messiah, he rebuked them and was driven from his home town (Lk. 4:28-29). Similarly, John rebuked Herod for his ungodly lifestyle;

but unlike Jesus who continued on his way, John's mission was coming to completion as he was locked up in prison and later beheaded for his proclamation of repentance (Lk. 3:20, Matt. 14:10).

Jesus continued on to Capernaum where he healed various kinds of illnesses, but as news of his healings spread, the people began looking for him even at daybreak as he sought a 'solitary place' (Lk. 4:42). The people came to him in order to have their temporal needs met, but Jesus pressed on towards Judea knowing that he needed to 'proclaim the good news of the kingdom of God' because that was why he had been sent (Lk. 4:42-43). Meeting practical needs was secondary to the gospel.

The crowd continued to find Jesus but one day, as Jesus was standing by the Lake of Gennesaret he spotted some fisherman. They had been working hard all night to catch fish but they hadn't caught anything (Lk. 5:5). This was a day they might never forget as they were called by the Messiah to drop their nets and follow him (Lk. 5:10). These ordinary men would soon take the gospel message out to the nations and fish for people (Lk. 5:10). I remember the moment I heard and believed the gospel message; it was as if God found me in the wilderness; I was desperately lost and in need of a Saviour. I have not stopped following the Lord Jesus since then. Though I continue to stumble and stray from the path, I am confident that he is leading me home.

Prayer: *Heavenly Father, thank you that you enabled me to hear the voice of Jesus and believe that his Word is trustworthy and true. Thank you for healing me and allowing me to walk in your presence. Thank you for forgiving me and sending Jesus to be the gate through which I am able to come before you. Amen.*

My thoughts, feelings and questions from the readings...

_____

_____

_____

_____

_____

_____

_____

_____

_____

_____

_____

_____

_____

_____

31

Lost

Readings: Luke 10-12, Matthew 10, Acts 6-7

AFTER LEAVING EVERYTHING TO FOLLOW Jesus, the disciples spent three years listening to his teachings, witnessing his miracles and being prepared for the time when he would no longer be with them in body. They were given authority to drive out demons and heal every sickness and disease (Matt. 10:1). Jesus sent them out with a few instructions "do not go among the Gentiles or enter any town of the Samaritans. Go rather to the lost sheep of Israel. As you go, proclaim this message: 'the Kingdom of heaven has come near'. Heal the sick, raise the dead, cleanse those who have leprosy, drive out demons. Freely you have received; freely give" (Matt. 10:5-8).

Jesus gave them firm boundaries for their ministry - a job description. He went on to say "Do not get any gold or silver or copper to take with you in your belts- no bag for the journey or extra shirt or sandals or a staff, for the worker is worth his keep" (Matt. 10:9-10). He gave their positions value and worth. Next, he said "whatever town or village you enter, search there for some worthy person and stay at their house until you leave... If anyone will not welcome you or listen to your words, leave that home or town and shake the dust off your feet" (Matt. 10:11-14). Their responsibility was to speak God's word to those who would listen, those who would welcome them in. It was not their role to convert or coerce.

Jesus refused to sugar-coat the work ahead of them. He said: "I am sending you out like sheep among wolves", suffering is coming for those who partake in this ministry; they will be arrested, flogged, persecuted, hated and killed and yet he encouraged them to "stand firm to the end" for they would be saved (v22). They were to go out like servants (v24), without fear and acknowledge openly what they had learned and come to believe to be true in their hearts about Jesus (v26). Their message would bring division not peace amongst families (Matt. 10:34-35); it would bring cost and loss (v38). But though the cost might be great, and for some it may be too much to bear, he reminded them "whoever finds their life will lose it, and whoever loses their life for my sake will find it" (Matt. 10:39).

The word *life* in its usage in the text refers to the Greek word "psuché", which is the root of the English word for "psychology" - in other words Jesus is referring to the "self", the individual. This is a shocking statement in our current culture. It means that in order to serve the Lord Jesus wholeheartedly, to follow Christ, a person must lose their own desire for self-fulfilment. Instead of pursuing a life of individualism they are to become part of a community that lives to serve the Lord Jesus; to bring the message of the Kingdom to those who will listen. Of course, Jesus knows that when one is called and sent they will never imagine going back to their old way of living again. That is the beauty and miracle of the gospel when it is heard and sinks deep into one's heart. It changes desires and transforms lives.

Prayer: Heavenly Father, thank you that you called me, that you gave me a wonderful season to study your Word, to understand and listen to your teachings, to gaze in wonderment at your miracles. Father please send me out, give me great boldness to proclaim your Word from the rooftops to all who will listen. Please help me to follow you wholeheartedly, to give up my earthly selfish desires and to live a life serving you and your people. Amen.

My thoughts, feelings and questions from the readings…

_____

_____

_____

_____

_____

_____

_____

_____

_____

_____

_____

_____

_____

_____

32

Filled

A S THE WORD ABOUT JESUS gathered momentum, the crowd again began to follow Jesus because of the signs he had performed by healing the sick and as he sat with his disciples on a mountainside, he watched the crowd coming towards him. Anticipating their physical need for food, and knowing how to truly satisfy their insatiable hearts, he turned to his disciples to see what they would do. "Where shall we buy bread for these people to eat?" (Jn. 6:5). Philip answered "It would take more than half a year's wages to buy enough bread for each one to have a bite" (Jn. 6:7). Andrew was a little more resourceful and found a boy with five small barley loaves and two small fish but couldn't see how it would be able to feed the multitude (Jn. 6: 8-9).

It seemed an impossible task from the disciples' perspective, far too costly and beyond their capacity and yet Jesus again spoke and organised for the crowd to "sit down", then he took the loaves, gave thanks and distributed to those who were seated, as much as they wanted. He did the same with the fish. (Jn. 6: 8-11). There was an abundance of food, even leftovers which were gathered up (Jn. 6:13). Jesus's ministry was attracting the crowds but perhaps for the wrong reasons. The next day the crowd that witnessed the feeding of the multitude were wanting more from Jesus. They still saw Jesus as a means to provide for their physical needs but Jesus desired that they look to their spiritual poverty. He said "Do not work for food that spoils, but for food that endures to eternal life, which the Son of Man will give you" (Jn. 6:27).

Inquiring further they asked "What must we do to do the works God requires?" (Jn. 6:28). Again, the people thought that somehow, they could work for God's approval. And yet Jesus corrected their thinking: "The work of God is this: to believe in the one he has sent" (Jn. 6:29). Shockingly, they asked him "What sign then will you give that we may see it and believe you? What will you do?" (Jn. 6:30). They needed even more evidence in order to believe. Jesus recognised their disbelief and reminded them that even to believe in Jesus was a work of God, it is all by grace.

Jesus pointed to their history, their ancestors who ate manna in the wilderness and died and yet he offered them a new life there, living bread which had come down from heaven - God himself, available without cost to them. There was a mixed response there and the disciples grumbled, reminiscent of their ancestors, but Jesus continued to move their thinking from the physical. He said "The Spirit gives life; the flesh counts for nothing. The words I have spoken to you -they are full of the Spirit and life" (Jn. 6:63). This was too much for some and they could not accept his teaching - they turned back. But the Twelve remained with Peter acknowledging that Jesus held the words of eternal life (Jn. 6:68). In the final words of this chapter we are reminded that Jesus will be betrayed by one of his own disciples (Jn. 6:70-71). Jesus already knew who would believe in him, who would walk away and who would ultimately betray him.

Prayer: Heavenly Father, thank you for your wonderful provision of Jesus, the living bread. Thank you for enabling me to realise my poverty and hunger. Thank you for giving me food that satisfies and work that is enduring. Please open the hearts and minds of those who still do not understand your teaching and do not believe in Jesus. Please have mercy on them and send your Holy Spirit so that they may have life in your Son's name. Amen.

My thoughts, feelings and questions from the readings...

_____

_____

_____

_____

_____

_____

_____

_____

_____

_____

_____

_____

_____

33

Beautiful

Readings: Psalm 109, Isaiah 52, John 12-13

A S JESUS APPROACHED THE FINAL days of his life on earth he continued to teach and share his life with those closest to him. A week before the Passover Festival, Jesus visited Bethany to have dinner with his friend Lazarus (Jn. 12:1-2). Mary who had previously been encouraged by Jesus in her decision to sit at his feet and learn from him, took a bottle of expensive perfume and instinctively poured it on his feet (Jn. 12:3). A beautiful aroma filled the house, from the feet of Jesus, one who had come from the mountains to proclaim the good news (Isa. 52:7).

Judas reacted scathingly to her sacrifice, accusing her of neglecting the poor (Jn. 12:5). But Judas's heart was far from wanting to help the poor, he was a thief and soon he would trade his own soul (Jn. 12:6). Jesus had previously raised Lazarus to life and a crowd was gathering to see him. They were placing their trust in Jesus because of what he had done for Lazarus (Jn. 12:11). The chief priests and the teachers of the law were not only looking for a way 'to get rid of Jesus' but also Lazarus (Jn. 12:10, Lk. 22:2). Now in Jerusalem, seemingly the 'whole world' was following Jesus (Jn. 12:19) and we learn about the moment Satan entered Judas and waited for a time when he could hand Jesus over to them (Lk. 22:6).

Sin and human delight appeared to go hand in hand as they prepared to kill the one who had come to save them. The day arrived for the celebration of the Passover where the lamb would be sacrificed and eaten in the homes of the Jewish citizens of Jerusalem (Lk. 22:7). Jesus asked Peter and John to get things ready. A guest room was prepared and while they sat at the table with Jesus, he reminded them that this would be his last supper with them (Lk. 22:15-16). His time had come for the fulfilment of God's promises to Abraham. Following supper Jesus made his way to the Mount of Olives as he did every evening to pray (Lk. 21:37). This was the same place Zechariah had prophesied the Messiah would stand and battle the enemies of Israel (Zech. 14:3-4).

It was time for the people of Zion to awake. The Messiah was about to defeat their greatest enemy, sin. The next forty-eight hours would bring trial, death and suffering. But Gods' goodness to his people was coming. Jesus was going to raise himself from the dead just like he said he would.

Prayer: *Heavenly Father, thank you for sending your Son to do battle against our greatest enemies, sin and death. Thank you that you loved us so much that you would not allow us to endure the suffering that was required by your Law. Thank you that you have given me faith through the gift of your Holy Spirit to believe that Jesus is the promised Messiah, the Holy One of Israel who came to seek and to save the lost sheep of Israel and bring them home. Amen.*

My thoughts, feelings and questions from the readings...

_____

_____

_____

_____

_____

_____

_____

_____

_____

_____

_____

_____

_____

34

Go

Readings: Luke 24, Acts 4-5, Galatians 1-2

HE RESURRECTION AND ASCENSION OF Jesus and the coming of the Holy Spirit ushered in a new age for the disciples. The believers were united in 'heart and mind' (Acts 4:32). Filled with the power of the Holy Spirit they shared everything they had and there were no needy persons among them. There was a spirit of radical, sacrificial generosity, like Joseph, a Levite from Cyprus, who sold an entire field and brought the proceeds to the apostles' feet (Acts 4:34-37). They called him Barnabas, a man full of the Holy Spirit and utterly committed to missionary work, later becoming a prophet and teacher of the church in Antioch (Acts 13:1).

Barnabas was clearly growing in his faith and yet there were still moments where he was led astray. Years after his initial conversation Cephas, otherwise known as the apostle Peter went to Antioch and it was there that Paul opposed him to his face (Gal. 2:11). Although Peter had received the message of the gospel and was full of the Holy Spirit, he tended to judge other believers when they gathered together to eat. At times he would eat with the Gentiles but when members came from the 'circumcision group', he separated himself because he was afraid of them. Peter was a leader and so others joined him in this 'hypocrisy' and even Barnabas was led astray (Gal. 2:13). Paul could no longer be silent and watch this unfold so he said to Peter in front of them all "you are a Jew, yet you live like a Gentile and not like a Jew. How is it, then, that you force Gentiles to follow Jewish customs?" (Gal. 2:14).

In Peter's old life as a Jew he would never have eaten with a non-Jew (Gentile). In fact, their entire legal system was designed so that there would be a separation from the nations around them in order for them to be set apart. Circumcision was unique to the Jewish nation. The problem was, the 'circumcision group' were demanding that Gentile converts to Christianity be circumcised in order to belong. Paul stood up and defended the true gospel reminding them that "a person is not justified by the works of the law, but by faith in Jesus Christ" (Gal. 2:16a). Paul spoke of the new life he had been given "The life I now live in the body, I live by faith in the Son of God, who loved me and gave himself for me" (Gal. 2:20).

Peter needed reminding that years ago he preached of this new life too. It was Peter who said before the Sanhedrin "We must obey God rather than human beings!" (Acts 5:29). We continually need reminding of this new life that we have been called to live because, like Barnabas and Peter, we will be tempted to follow a false gospel, a gospel which is more about *us* than *Jesus*. That's why it is so important for Christians to meet together regularly; to encourage one another; to rebuke when necessary when we see a fellow believer following a different message apart from the gospel; and to remind one another to keep speaking and to "tell people all about this new life" (Acts 5:20).

Prayer: *Heavenly Father, thank you for sending your Holy Spirit which enables your people to preach and proclaim this new life in Jesus Christ. Thank you for the lives of Barnabas, Peter and Paul and the way they committed their lives to serving and following your Son. Thank you for the many churches they established to enable Christianity to become established in the Roman Empire. Please help me to commit to my fellow brothers and sisters in my church family in which you have placed me. Please help me to show radical generosity in meeting their needs and help me live a life of faith in Jesus Christ alone and speak about that life to others. Amen.*

35

Hear

Readings: Acts 8-11, John 16-17, Galatians 3-4

F OLLOWING THE DEATH OF STEPHEN, a great persecution broke out against the church in Jerusalem and many believers were scattered throughout Judea and Samaria. Nothing could stop the gospel because wherever they went, they would preach the word and proclaim the good news about Jesus the Messiah (Acts 8:5). After hearing that Samaria had accepted the message, they sent Peter and John to Samaria to pray for the new believers that they would receive the Holy Spirit and they did (Acts 8:17). Peter travelled the country visiting the Lord's people, healing and raising the dead in Jesus's name.

Peter had continued to flourish in his faith since being filled with the Holy Spirit at Pentecost and even though God was working miraculous signs through him, he still had much to learn. By God's providence, he stayed for some time in the home of a tanner name Simon in Joppa - the same city to which Jonah ran to find a ship to Tarshish when God called him to go to Nineveh (Jnh. 1:3). Peter ate and drank and slept in the same house as a man who worked with dead animals. Tanners were despised in Ancient times; they were usually housed in isolation from the villages because the animal skins were soaked in urine and dung. Imagine large vats of animal brains and decaying flesh fermenting for weeks!

Despite the cultural and societal differences, Simon welcomed Peter into his home. Peter grew up understanding that if he were to have contact with anything dead, whether animal or man, this would make him unclean. Therefore, the fact that he had earlier prayed for a woman who had died and was now surrounded by carcasses was evidence of a life-altering change in worldview. Peter's life had undergone a transformation yet he was still holding on to Jewish ideas about food. It was in Joppa that God reminded Peter that all food was clean, and that the old food laws had been fulfilled (Acts 10:15).

That moment was life transforming for Peter and God's word was confirmed when he met in the home of a Gentile believer, Cornelius, the following day. Peter had learned that his faith in Christ was not just for him and his fellow Jewish believers, it was for the Gentiles too. In fact, it was for all the nations. He said "I now realise how true it is that God does not show favouritism but accepts from every nation the one who fears him and does what is right" (Acts 10:34-35) - those who trust in Jesus Christ. This is the good news! This is the part of God's promise to Abraham that all nations would be blessed through his offspring (Gen. 22:18) - that includes you and me.

Prayer: *Heavenly Father, thank you that you included all the nations in your plan of salvation. Thank you for the way you taught Peter and changed his life so that your gospel could travel out to Judea and Samaria. Thank you that you send us to places and put us in situations that we would never have imagined for the growth of your Kingdom. Thank you for changing our thoughts and rigid ways of living. Thank you that you are continually renewing and teaching me through your Word and to others who preach in your name in my hearing. Amen.*

My thoughts, feelings and questions from the readings...

_____

_____

_____

_____

_____

_____

_____

_____

_____

_____

_____

_____

36

Breath

Readings: Acts 17, Psalm 150, Galatians 5-6

WITH PAUL'S MISSIONARY EFFORTS EXPANDING in Gentile territory he spent time in Thessalonica reasoning from the Scriptures with both Jews and God-fearing Greeks (Acts 17:1). For three days he met with them in the synagogue and some Jews were persuaded and joined them as well as some Greeks and a few prominent women (Acts 17:2-4). But jealousy arose amongst some other Jews and they set out to persecute the believers (vv.5-9). They stirred up trouble and attempted to cause division. Paul and Silas slipped away to Berea in the night and met with the Berean Jews in the synagogue (v10). They received the message with enthusiasm and studied their Scriptures to see if what Paul preached, was true, many of them believed as well as prominent Greek women and men (Acts 17:11-12).

But the same Jews in Thessalonica found out that Paul was preaching the word of God and some went to Berea and stirred up trouble there too (v13). The believers protected Paul and sent him to the coast to wait for Silas and Timothy. As Paul waited for them in Athens he was 'distressed' as he realised the depth of the city's idolatry. He reasoned again in the synagogues with Jews and Greeks and those in the marketplace (Acts 17:14-17). Paul was placed in the midst of a polytheistic culture that loved to puff themselves up with ideas about life and Paul had brought a new idea into their midst. They were eager to learn more about his 'strange ideas', there appeared to be a genuine openness to exchanging ideas (Acts 17:20- 21).

Paul was invited to attend a meeting at the Areopagus, otherwise known as a "big piece of rock". In more modern times the rocky outcrop became known as 'Mars Hill' after the Roman God of War. Ironically, Paul was preparing to battle the existing thoughts of a culture that was wired for religion. Paul began his proclamation commending their 'religious' life (Acts 17:22) and yet quickly called out their ignorance (Acts 17:23). Paul spoke from his listeners' worldview quoting the very people they esteemed as prophets carefully weaving ideas that they had heard into what God had already written in the Scriptures. He used their own arguments to debunk the idea that God can be found in a temple or contained in gold or silver or stone made by human hands (Acts 17:29). It is God who gives everyone life and he did this so that people would seek him which the Greeks were attempting to do but just hadn't found the right way. Paul corrected their foolish thinking and pointed out their need for repentance before the coming judgement (Acts 17:30-31).

Christian or non-Christian we have been made in God's image; we're wired for worship. If we're not worshipping the one true God, we're worshipping a false one. The Triune God trumps Zeus because he is the God who made the world and everything in it! He is the Lord of heaven and earth and he doesn't need humans but in his great love he gave everyone 'life and breath' (Acts 17:25). The Psalmist understood the greatness of our God. He sang that our only response as his creation is to praise him; "let everything that has breath praise the LORD" (Ps. 150:6). How awesome is the God whom we serve!

Prayer: *Heavenly Father, thank you that you made yourself known to mankind through the Scriptures. Thank you that creation points to you and that you have given us a desire to want to know you. Thank you that you sustain the universe and that you cannot be contained in a building or precious metal made by man. Father thank you for Jesus, the giver of life. Please let me praise you forever! Amen.*

My thoughts, feelings and questions from the readings...

_____

_____

_____

_____

_____

_____

_____

_____

_____

_____

_____

_____

_____

FORTY YEARS OF THANKFULNESS

37

Living

Readings: Acts 18, Isaiah 64, 1 Corinthians 15

A FTER LEAVING ATHENS, PAUL HEADED to Corinth. I personally love Paul's letters to the Corinthian church. They are packed full of practical advice for dealing with issues in the church and these issues are still being experienced today. They remind and encourage us that even the earliest believers struggled in their Christian communities. The beginning of the church in Corinth arose through great suffering. Paul originally worked alongside fellow believers Aquila and Priscilla as a tentmaker and later once Silas and Timothy joined them, he was able to devote himself to preaching and testifying to the Jews that Jesus was the Messiah (Acts 18:5).

But the Jews continued to oppose him to the point of heaping abuse on him and he was moved to turn his efforts to the Gentiles (Acts 18:6). He first visited the house of Titius Justus, and many Corinthians believed that night and were baptised (Acts 18:7-8). The Lord continued to encourage and affirm his work amongst the Corinthians urging him to keep speaking and not be afraid for God was with him (Acts 18:9-10). It was in Corinth that we first meet Sosthenes, a synagogue leader who was physically beaten by a crowd when the Jews were unable to persecute Paul (Acts 18:17). Paul mentioned him as a brother (1 Cor. 1:1) and it seems as though he joined Paul in his missionary work in Ephesus, a likely place where he wrote these letters.

Whilst Paul was away from the church in Corinth, doubt arose in the church over the resurrection (1 Cor. 15:12). These same questions arise in our culture today as we ponder the impossibility of a man being raised from the dead. Paul answered their questions by first reminding them of the original message he proclaimed to them, whom they had trusted in. He reminded them that Jesus *is* the Messiah, that he had died and risen to life and that there were witnesses to this, over five hundred, most of whom were still alive at the time of Paul's letter (1 Cor. 15:3-6). The message about Jesus *is* trustworthy and you believed it when you heard it, therefore, do not depart from it!

Paul spoke to their questions about the resurrection, that the hope of the Christian faith hinges on the resurrection (1 Cor. 15:16-17). Finally, Paul reminded them that their heavenly bodies will be glorious, unlike anything humans have experienced but this victory over death can only be achieved through the Lord Jesus Christ (1 Cor. 56-57). He concluded in this chapter by reminding them to "stand firm" and keep serving the Lord Jesus (1 Cor. 58). They are to continue to be unmoved, steadfast and abound in God's work.

Prayer: *Heavenly Father, thank you that the message I first heard about your son Jesus is trustworthy. Thank you that through your Holy Spirit you have produced steadfastness in me. Please help me to continue to believe the gospel message in the Bible and abound in your work fully, that I might give glory to you in every part of my life and that I might be unmoved as I hold out for the coming hope of eternal glory. Amen.*

My thoughts, feelings and questions from the readings...

_____

_____

_____

_____

_____

_____

_____

_____

_____

_____

_____

_____

_____

_____

_____

FORTY YEARS OF THANKFULNESS

38

Father

Readings: Acts 27-28, Psalm 62, Romans 1-4

L IFE IN THE CAPITAL, ANCIENT Rome, in the first century, was a bustling centre of political, educational and societal activity. It's possible that Aquila and Priscilla first heard the gospel in Rome before they were expelled under the Roman Emperor Claudius (Acts 18:2). Perhaps it was during this time as they shared their lives that Paul's heart enlarged for the believers in Rome. In the beginning of Paul's letter to those loved by God in Rome he mentioned that 'their faith is being reported all over the world' (Rom. 1:8). He had been praying for them and hoped that 'the way may be opened' for him to visit them (Rom. 1:10). It was always Paul's intention to visit Rome (Acts 19:21) but it was confirmed by God after he appeared before the Sanhedrin (Acts 23:10). It was the following night that the Lord stood close to Paul and said "Take courage! As you have testified about me in Jerusalem, so you must also testify in Rome" (Acts 23:11).

Under guard, Paul stayed in Rome for two years in his own rented house and welcomed those who came to see him. He continued to preach and teach about the kingdom of God that Jesus proclaimed (Acts 28:31).

Paul's purpose for wanting to visit them was to strengthen, encourage and be encouraged (Rom. 1:11-12). Believers in Rome were amidst a culture that prized achievement. For the Jewish Christians, their own worldview was steeped in Old Testament history of God's chosen people and it was difficult for them to grasp that God would act in saving *all* people.

Paul reminded them that all humanity had fallen short of God's glory, all had sinned and were under God's judgement (Rom. 3:11), but salvation was available to all. The Law cannot save them, it is only *in* the gospel that salvation is available to all who believe (Rom. 1:16). Paul demonstrated this by giving the example of Abraham in whom they trusted; he was declared righteous by God before he was circumcised. Therefore, it was by grace that Abraham was saved; the uncircumcised could be declared righteous too. Paul was hoping to broaden their view and see that Abraham was promised to be the 'father of many nations' (Rom. 4:17). Paul explained the gospel message- that the power of the gospel was found in the death and resurrection of Jesus which provided the justification for new life (Rom. 4:25).

Prayer: Heavenly Father, thank you for the hope of the resurrection. Thank you for giving me the gift of believing that you raised Jesus from the dead. Thank you for declaring me righteous before you. Father thank you for the provision of Abraham and the model of a faithful life he provided. But ultimately Father thank you that Jesus was able to fulfil the promises made to Abraham thousands of years ago so that I may be counted among his offspring. Amen.

My thoughts, feelings and questions from the readings...

_____

_____

_____

_____

_____

_____

_____

_____

_____

_____

_____

_____

_____

39

Treasure

Readings: 1-2 Timothy, Psalm 135, Romans 5-8

PAUL'S FINAL LETTER TO TIMOTHY was filled with deep emotion. He was thankful to God for Timothy, he remembered the tears Timothy shed and longed to see him again so that he could be filled with joy (2 Tim. 1:3-4). He was reminded about Timothy's faith that first lived in his grandmother, then his mother and now Timothy. This family was certainly under the hand of God and Timothy was being prepared for ministry long before he met Paul. One can only imagine the treasure trove of knowledge passed down to Timothy in those times as a child and the intimate moments watching his mother and grandmother pray. This closeness had also formed between Paul and Timothy. This was Paul's final handing down of knowledge to his spiritual son and it was treasure-filled indeed.

Knowing that Paul was imprisoned and near the end of his earthly life would have no doubt shaken Timothy's faith and yet Paul's passion for the Lord Jesus was evident as he reminded Timothy to "fan into flame the gift of God" (2 Tim. 1:6). My littlest one delights in throwing dried up leaves onto a campfire-he shouts out "More flame! More flame!"

and the fire burns bright again. Paul said to Timothy, keep asking for kindling; the free gift of grace given by God, the indwelling of the Holy Spirit, God himself (2 Tim. 1:7). The same message given to the believers in Rome was given to Timothy 'do not be ashamed' of the gospel because it is the power of God for salvation (Rom. 1:16-17, 2 Tim. 1:8-9) - These same words were spoken to Paul by the Lord Jesus at various points in his ministry when people started deserting him (2 Tim. 4:17).

Paul reminds us that standing firm in Christ involves hardship and loss, opposition and attack but it also means a crown of righteousness, a race run well and fellowship with God himself. It is good to stop and reflect at points along our Christian lives and ask ourselves "how are we running the race?" "Are we running for ourselves or for and with Christ?" "Are we enduring suffering for the sake of Christ or living in fear of failure?". These are good questions to consider as we pursue a godly life in Christ.

Prayer: Heavenly Father, thank you for the saints that have led the way in showing us what it means to live a godly life in Christ. Thank you for Paul and the way he lived his life for your glory. Thank you for Timothy and his mother and grandmother who guarded the faith and passed it on to the next generation. Please help me to run the Christian race in such a way that gives glory to you. Amen.

My thoughts, feelings and questions from the readings...

_____

_____

_____

_____

_____

_____

_____

_____

_____

_____

_____

_____

_____

FORTY YEARS OF THANKFULNESS

40

Everlasting

Readings: 1-2 Peter, Psalm 118, Romans 9-12

WHILST WE HAVE SPENT SOME time tracing Paul's life from Jerusalem out to the Gentile territories, Peter continued to preach and teach with a focus on the Jews. Peter was the first of the disciples to acknowledge Jesus as the Messiah, yet we learn that even Peter had abandoned Christ in the lead-up to the Crucifixion. With the gift of the Holy Spirit, Peter was equipped to live his life boldly fishing for men just as Jesus had called him to do. Peter's first letter in the New Testament is addressed to the 'elect': people known by God but considered strange and foreign on earth (1 Pet. 1:1). Likely to have been written under Emperor Nero, this was the first official time Christians were persecuted by the Roman Empire during the period 62-64AD.

Peter reminded them that they had been chosen to be obedient to Jesus Christ (1 Pet. 1:2). He went on to give thanks to God for his mercy, giving his people new life and an everlasting inheritance (1 Pet. 1:4). He reminded them that even though they were suffering all kinds of trials, good things were coming and their faith would be proved genuine if they persevered. He commended them for their faith and love for Jesus 'though they have not seen him', the mark of this is a heart filled with 'inexpressible and glorious joy' (1 Pet. 1:8-9). He reminded them of the sufferings of the Messiah and the glory that followed. Because of this he said: 'set your hope on the grace to be brought to you when Jesus Christ is revealed at his coming' (1 Pet. 1:13). While you wait for Jesus to return for the final time; 'be holy' (1 Pet. 1:16). Then he spoke to the momentary life as foreigners, to live in reverent fear (1 Pet. 1:17). Peter reminded them of the costly sacrifice God made to redeem them 'the precious blood of Christ, a lamb without blemish or defect' (1 Pet. 1:19).

Peter commended them for obeying the truth, evident in their great love for one another, but he urged them to love even more deeply (1 Pet. 1:22). This type of love is reserved specifically for Christian believers and it takes effort to love like this. It is an active, moving love. It means to be fervently committed to the people God has placed in our local church, even if they are unlike us, even if it is costly, even if it seems that they do not love us back. Love with an enduring love that God has already modelled to us in sending Jesus. This type of love endures and gives glory to God and has eternal value. This type of love is everlasting.

Prayer: *Heavenly Father, thank you for the body of believers you have placed us amongst to serve. Thank you that the mystery of the church is the way you mature and make us holy. Father thank you for giving me this time delighting in your Word and helping me to practise thankfulness rather than grumbling. Thank you for renewing and strengthening me in my love for you, your people and for those who are still lost. Father please continue your work in your people so that we reflect your glory as we place our hope in the rock of our salvation, our Lord Jesus Christ. In his wonderful name. Amen.*

My thoughts, feelings and questions from the readings...

_____

_____

_____

_____

_____

_____

_____

_____

_____

_____

_____

_____

_____

_____

FORTY YEARS OF THANKFULNESS

www.ingramcontent.com/pod-product-compliance
Lightning Source LLC
Chambersburg PA
CBHW051425090426

42737CB00014B/2834